10 STEPS TO EARNING
AWESOME GRADES
(while studying less)

THOMAS FRANK

CONTENTS

A NOTE ABOUT LINKS

The digital versions of this book link to several apps, websites, and extended online resources that you might find helpful.

Through extensive testing, though, I've found these links don't work on paper no matter how hard I jab at them with my iPad stylus, and now there are dents in my kitchen table.

So to keep your kitchen table dent-free, I've created a centralized list of all the links in the book. Whenever you see <u>underlined text</u>, you can find the site it links to over at collegeinfogeek.com/booklinks.

INTRODUCTION

There is a goat icon on the cover of this book because putting it there made it easy to start this introduction. Also, goats are hilarious.

Moreover, goats are really smart, and they'd probably get damn good grades if they stopped yelling long enough to think about goat school.

Enough about goat grades, though - this book is meant to help you improve *your* grades.

A couple facts to put out there before we begin:

First, for most students, my opinion on grades is that they do **not** need to be perfect. After you define your goals, you'll find that your coursework is not a magical Hogwarts train that will take you to them.

It'll help, but alone it's inadequate. Focus on getting *good* grades while also gaining skills outside of class, building things, doing extracurriculars, making connections and - yes - making time to have fun. Even if it's just playing 10 minutes of *Goat Simulator* (don't worry, that's the last goat joke).

Second, the main point of this book is to help you earn better grades, but the almost-as-important sub-focus is to *cut down your study time*. It's my aim here to give you tools and tactics that help you perform better in **less time**. There's a neat little equation I invented below that explains this a little better.

The Study Time Equation

What are the factors that actually go into earning awesome grades? In my mind, the best way to look at this is to envision the final goal not as the *tangible reward* - the grade - but rather as the *state of being* you want to achieve.

I define this as **Desired Preparedness**. This applies to any class you're in - or, to get more granular, to any specific exam/assignment/project.

The grade is simply a result you can use to quantify your desired preparedness. Once you've set that goal, there are four factors that will go into achieving it.

1. Class Time
2. Learning Quality
3. Study Time
4. Study Efficiency

Given those factors, here's the initial form of the equation:

$$\left(\frac{Class}{Time} \cdot \frac{Learning}{Quality}\right) + \left(\frac{Study}{Time} \cdot \frac{Study}{Efficiency}\right) = \frac{Desired}{Preparedness}$$

Pretty simple, no? Now we just do some algebraic fiddling to solve for Study Time:

$$\frac{Study}{Time} = \frac{\frac{Desired}{Preparedness} - \left(\frac{Class}{Time} \cdot \frac{Learning}{Quality}\right)}{Study \quad Efficiency}$$

To decrease (this), increase (these)

Assuming you're committed to attending all your classes, Class Time is fixed. It's a constant. If you've already set a goal for Desired Preparedness, that's fixed for now as well.

This means you've got two variables to work with: **Learning Quality** and **Study Efficiency**. To decrease the amount of time you need to spend studying, increase either of them. Or be a baller and increase both.

Book Overview

The rest of this book is dedicated to giving you strategies and tactics to do just that. I've organized the book into **10 steps**, each of which covers a different skill area:

- Paying Better Attention in Class
- Taking Effective Notes
- Getting More Out of Your Textbooks
- Planning Efficiently
- Building Your Optimal Study Environment
- Staying Organized
- Defeating Procrastination
- Studying Smarter
- Writing Better Papers
- Making Group Projects Suck Less

I called them 10 steps, but you should actually think of them as levels in a *Mega Man* game - you can take them on in any order. Just as you get new power-ups and weapons after each level in the game, you'll get stronger after completing each step here.

It doesn't actually matter which one you start with - if you've got a particular problem area, skip to that section and start implementing the tips you find there before you try to load everything else into your brain.

The words of CD Baby founder Derek Sivers fit perfectly here:

"Ideas are just a multiplier of execution."

Multiply anything by zero and you get… zero. You'll be a lot better off if you just read one step of this book and put it into **action** than if you read the whole thing and proceed to do jack.

Keeping that in mind, let's take on the first robot master…er, step.

STEP 1: PAY BETTER ATTENTION IN CLASS

Since your Class Time is a constant rather than a variable, I think it makes sense to prioritize Learning Quality first. The more you can learn while you're part of your professor's captive audience, the less work your Study Efficiency will have to do later when you'd rather be hanging with friends and playing *Fibbage* (the best party game ever, I might add)

The first step to upgrading your learning quality is deceptively simple: **Pay better attention in class**.

This is one of those "easier said than done" pieces of advice; semesters are long and classes constantly wage a war of attrition against your motivation levels. These strategies will help you weather the storm.

Don't Overload the System

I had a professor in my MIS program who was quite the character. In addition to praising "the Google" at least twice a week and sending students on extra-credit missions that involved photographing Cabbage Patch kids in weird locations - like Intel's chip manufacturing facility - he'd also end every class by saying,

> *"Don't overload the system!"*

The system he was referring to is your brain, but I'm going to take it a step further and define the system as your body.

This isn't a huge stretch, actually; Elliot Hulse, a strongman/fitness personality with over 1 million subscribers on YouTube, has a key philosophy that **your body is your mind**.

Your mind does all the work involved in earning awesome grades, and the performance of that mind is dependent on the state of your body. As Elliot's YouTube intro video eloquently puts it:

> *"The most important part of the game is your game piece!"*

7

I go to the bookstore and look at the college prep section a lot (it's an upgraded version of a motivational technique called *visualization*) since I want to see my work there some day. Almost every college success book I thumb through mentions health somewhere...

...but it still bears repeating. Why?

The truth is that most of us are like the kid who goes to karate class and wants to learn flying tornado kicks before mastering proper balance. We want little tricks, hacks, and tactics that promise to make our lives better.

However, all the little mind hacks and study tricks in the world won't help you if you're constantly suffering from bad health due to poor nutrition, lack of sleep, and inadequate exercise.

Picture two ninjas: One keeps his body in top form and practices every day, but his master's a hard-ass and only lets him fight with his bare hands.

The other actually isn't a ninja at all - he's just an unhealthy anime addict yelling quotes from Naruto and holding a $5,000 katana bought for him by his rich dad.

Who's going to win that fight?

All this is an elaborate way of trying to convince you to make your health **priority #1**. Be deliberate about:

- Eating healthy 90% of the time
- Working out regularly - this can be fun exercise; join an intramural sport or get addicted to DDR like me!
- Getting enough sleep - at least 6 hours a night

If you want to learn how to do these things properly, check out my friend Steve Kamb's site Nerd Fitness. There's an article there called _A College Guide to Eating Healthy_ that might be a good place to start.

Sit Up Front and Be Present

Tap. Tap tap tap.

I woke up from my pleasant nap at the back of the huge lecture hall to find a really attractive girl tapping on my shoulder. "Maybe she'll be down to play Crash Team Racing with me," says my brain.

Then she hands me a Red Bull.

I guess she was paid to hand out energy drinks to sleepy students in class - either way, I didn't make a Crash Racing friend that day. I also didn't learn anything in that Econ 101 class.

Fast forward a semester, and I'm in my Stat 226 class. I am in the front row, about 6 feet away from the professor's purse. I think I can see a Power Bar sticking out of it. I kind of want it.

No matter, though - my mind is focused only on what's being presented (mainly because I know I'm screwed if I don't catch it. Stat is hard.) The only things on my desk are my notebook, calculator, and elbow. When class ends, I've filled five pages in my notebook with new statistics concepts that I *actually understand.* Also, I have not fallen asleep once, even though this is an 8 A.M. class.

See the difference? Stat is better than Econ because it doesn't give you false hope for making new Crash Racing friends.

I kid, I kid. The real difference is that sitting up front and making a *deliberate effort* to be present actually does help your focus, attention, and energy levels. And it all starts with choosing that row the moment you walk into the classroom.

Come Prepared

Every teacher you have ever had has told you to come prepared to class. I'm not going to pretend that I'm giving you some new piece of advice just by telling you to do it.

What I *do* want to mention here is that you can become better at doing this, because none of us is perfect at it. We all forget things - and when we forget things, we create **friction** that impedes our willpower to remain fully engaged in class.

So, to make sure you're prepared in class as much as possible, create a **mindfulness habit**. To me, being mindful means regularly considering the things that your life, and your goals, depend on - especially those that lie outside the current moment.

For instance, a non-mindful student would only think to start looking for an apartment one, maybe two months before he's supposed to move. A mindful student, on the other hand, would have asked landlords a year in advance what the best time to start looking is, learned it was 7–8 months beforehand, and then started his search at that time.

Likewise, a mindful student plans for the next day each night, and thinks about what needs to be in her bag for that day. She makes sure her laptop is charged if it needs to be, and checks to see that the right notebooks are in her bag. She makes sure any files she needs are in Dropbox instead of sitting on her desktop, unable to be accessed.

If you find that you're not as mindful as you'd like to be, an easy solution is to create a reminder, such as:

1. A note by your door or on your desk
2. A recurring daily task in your to-do app
3. An alarm on your phone

Anything that can trigger your mindfulness habit will work; eventually, you'll start anticipating it, and later you won't even need it.

Get Help from Your Professor (The Right Way)

Your professors want (in most cases) to help you, so you should definitely take advantage of their office hours if you ever have problems understanding the material in a class.

Not only will you get the help you need, but you'll also start building a relationship with that professor. This can be incredibly useful down the line, in addition to just being a generally cool thing to do.

When it comes to getting academic help, however, you should use the **Corson Technique**. Dale Corson, the 8th dean of Cornell University (the birthplace of the famous Cornell note-taking system), once remarked that students in engineering and science programs often have to work through a complex idea one sentence at a time in order to "crack" it.

If comprehension doesn't come even at this granular

level of study, it's time to ask the professor for help. However, Corson advises,

"Before you do, ask yourself this question:
What is it that I don't understand?*"*

What he means is that you should never go to your professor, open the book and, with a "general sweep of the hand" say that you don't understand what you're reading.

Rather, when you go for help, you should be able to show the professor all that you do understand up to an exact point – and even show what you understand afterwards.

By doing this, you show the professor that you've really wrestled with the problem. Doing this has several benefits:

- You save the professor's time and help them understand the exact context of your problem
- The professor knows that you actually give a damn and now will have a much better impression of you
- By really going to intellectual combat on the problem, you very well might solve it yourself before you need to ask

A programmer named Matt Ringel wrote a <u>blog post</u> a while back about an unwritten law at his company called the **"15 Minute Rule."** This is very similar to the Corson Technique, and gives some more specific guidance on how to act when you're stuck on a tough problem:

1. When you get stuck, push yourself to solve the problem for *15 more minutes.*
2. During that 15 minutes, document everything you do, keeping in mind that someone else will need those details if they're going to help you.
3. After that time, if you're still stuck, you must ask for help.

This rule is summed up in the mantra:

"First you must try; then you must ask."

If you dig into some of articles on College Info Geek (my website), you'll notice that I often talk about the importance of becoming a **Solution Finder**. To me, this is someone who knows how and where to search for answers to tough problems - and, more importantly, is *willing to do it*.

Becoming a Solution Finder will help you immensely in your college career; it'll build habits that'll enable you to find answers and solve problems that other people can't. However, there's a balance to be struck;

eventually, you should be willing to seek the help of your professors when you've exhausted your other options.

Keep Those Hands Moving

This last tip stems from an observation I made early on in college: Being an **active participant** is almost always better than being a **passive observer**.

We're more easily able to remember things that we actively participated in than things we were merely exposed to. When it comes to lecture-style classes, the best ways to be active are to speak up in class discussions and to **take lots of notes**.

Going back to my Statistics class - because I was constantly taking notes, my attention was almost always focused on the professor and the material. In other classes, my commitment to taking notes wasn't as strong, and as a result, I'd often find my attention directed to less useful things like reading old BOFH stories.

Forcing yourself to take notes can be hard, though - so you've got to turn it into a habit. To do that, you could:

- Form a study group and compare notes on a regular basis

- Use a habit-tracking tool like Habitica or Lift (more about Habitica - my tool of choice - later in the book)
- Elevate the importance of your notes...

...which I did in my first Management Information Systems class. How? **I made them public.**

That first MIS class was all about learning tons of facts and details about information systems, so I took all my notes in Evernote using the Outline Method. Evernote has a feature that lets you share a public link to a notebook, so that's what I did - and I posted the link in the Blackboard chatroom for the class.

I'm not sure how many people actually used my notes, but it didn't matter - in my mind, I had elevated my importance in the class beyond that of an isolated student, and as a result I placed added importance on the quality of my notes.

You don't have to go that far, but you should still find a way to build a habit that keeps those hands moving when you're in class.

So now that you've committed to taking notes in every class (even if you don't feel like it), the next step will teach you *how to take those notes*.

STEP 2: TAKE MORE EFFECTIVE NOTES

Your notes are your method of taking the information that you're exposed to and recording it in a form that makes sense to you. When you do this, you learn more effectively. Also, you keep margins nearby for spontaneous drawings of those weird "S" things - or elaborately drawn out Mario levels if you're me.

In this step, I'll teach you what I know about taking **better** notes - notes that focus on *learning* rather than simply recording, that cut down on the processing you have to do after class, and that enable you to study more efficiently.

Five Excellent Note-Taking Methods

There are many ways of taking notes, one of which is dipping your entire head in ink and slamming it on your notebook, then making mental associations between what you're learning in class and specific features of the resulting picture, which probably looks like a rejected Rorschach test card at this point.

Unfortunately, the subsequent amnesia makes this a less-than-stellar method. I know you're dying to test it for yourself, but trust me - use one of these five systems instead.

Note: Books aren't a good format for images, but you can find visual examples of all of these in <u>my video on note-taking systems.</u>

The Outline Method

Aside from just mindlessly writing your notes out in paragraph form, the Outline Method is probably the simplest note-taking method that you could use. To use it, you just create bullet lists out of the lecture material or book you're reading.

- Main ideas are at the top level
- Supporting details become nested
  - Eventually you build an organized, hierarchical outline of the material
- This is pretty meta

I have a habit of reading a book for at least 15 minutes a day, and whenever I finish a chapter, I immediately go over to Evernote and type out some notes on what I read. When I do this the Outline Method is my system of choice.

While some of the other methods I'll be going over offer certain benefits for learning, I find that this method is perfect for recording a concise picture of the entire book without losing any important details. Also, if you prefer to take your notes on a computer, the Outline Method is one of the easiest to use.

The only problem with the Outline Method lies in how easily it lends itself to **mindless note-taking** - that is, simply recording the lecture material without really thinking about it or trying to put it in your own words. I've definitely been guilty in the past of sitting in certain classes and trying to note down every detail the professor says without really putting in the mental effort to learn.

The Cornell Method

I'd be surprised if you've never heard of this system before, though you may not know exactly how to use it. The Cornell Method was invented by Walter Pauk - the man who wrote the excellent textbook *How to Study in College* - and is designed to cut down on the amount of time you need to spend processing your notes after class before you can properly study them.

To take notes in the Cornell style, you divide your paper into three sections:

1. The Cue column
2. The Note-taking column
3. The Summary column

The Note-taking column will be the most familiar to you, as it just contains the notes you take during class. You can use any style you want, though in most cases people will use the Outline Method.

As you take your notes, you'll use the Cue column to formulate questions based on main ideas and important details from the Note-taking column. Once class is over, you should immediately write a small summary of what was presented in the Summary column.

By doing this, you're processing your notes for efficient study *while you're still in class*. When it comes time to actually study them, you'll find that you're already halfway to creating a great study guide, as you've already written down questions. You should also have a clearer understanding of the material already, since you took the time to summarize it.

The Mind Map Method

Mind mapping is a fantastic method for creating a tree of connected ideas, and I find that creating mind maps helps me to better flesh out ideas I want to write about. They're a great way to visualize a lot of information.

To create a mind map, start with a single "umbrella" term in the middle of your page. Then, start branching out from it by drawing lines and writing down words that flesh out that main idea.

Mind maps are very visual, so you should experiment with using different colors, drawing pictures next to your terms, and doing other things that help you understand and remember the information more clearly.

You don't have to use paper for your mind maps, either. While I prefer doing it that way, there are plenty of apps that let you make mind maps on your computer; my favorite is Coggle, which is a free web app that has a lot of convenient keyboard shortcuts for creating your maps.

For me, mind maps are best used when I'm trying to get a clear picture of all the details underneath a certain topic. I'm not so fond of using them when taking notes during classes, since I often like to create diagrams, write down more detailed blocks that don't always fit nicely into map nodes, etc.

But what if you want to integrate small mind maps into your notes? Can you create a hybrid system? Yes you can, and it's…

The Flow Method

Your brain stores information in a messy web of tangled facts, ideas, memories, and references. The structured hierarchy of Outline-style or Mind Mapped notes doesn't exactly represent how that content lives in your head.

Enter the Flow Method of taking notes. This method was created by Scott Young, a writer who is best known for going through a self-directed version of MIT's entire computer science curriculum in just one year. Scott takes in information using a technique he called **holistic learning**. This technique emphasizes learning in a style that mirrors your brain - creating interconnected webs of information (or "constructs"), visualizing things, and avoiding rote memorization.

The Flow Method is one of the cornerstones of holistic learning. Most other note-taking systems are based on hierarchy - as I illustrated in the section on the Outline Method, you put main terms at the top and nest related details directly under them. Mind maps are similar; the main term goes in the middle, and details branch out from there.

Conversely, Flow notes are meant to be an on-paper representation of your **mental picture** of a subject. When you take notes in this way, you're transcribing them in a completely original way instead of simply copying down what's presented in lecture. It's *very* difficult to become a mindless copying zombie when you're taking Flow notes, which is something that can't be said for the Outline Method.

> *"Flow-based notetaking is a creative process, not a recording process. Instead of just writing down what the professor argues, you're also going to come up with your own ideas, examples, and connections." - <u>Scott Young</u>*

The main goal of Flow-based note-taking is to help you **learn the material once**. By taking notes in this way, you should be able to actually integrate new facts into your existing body of knowledge the first time you process them, rather than having to go back later to study them a second time.

So, how do you **actually take** Flow-based notes? Here are the basics:

- Connect terms and ideas with arrows
- Deliberately write things down in your own words
- Create *backlinks* - links ideas back to related terms and details mentioned earlier in the lecture

This style of note-taking is probably the hardest to perfect, as it's very personal and requires you to think about your notes in a very different way than you're probably used to. If it's a style you want to pick up, give it a good few tries before writing it off.

Also, recognize that Flow-based note-taking isn't perfect for every subject; as Scott Young emphasizes, it's best for subjects where the ideas are easily connected to other ideas. For very detail-dense classes where the material doesn't easily form a dense web of connections, a more hierarchical system will probably help you capture all the information you'll need to study more effectively.

The "Write on the Slides" Method

If your professor is nice enough to provide the lecture slides to you before they're actually shown in class, then printing them out and taking notes right on them can be an excellent method of note-taking.

I call this the "lazy man's approach to note-taking," but in reality it's just efficient; if 80% of the information is already available for you to take home, then you can save a lot of time by simply adding personal notes and references on top of it instead of going through the effort of writing your notes from scratch.

One nice feature of this "system" is that it gives you

something similar to a **timeline** of the lecture. Since the slides are usually presented in a linear fashion, you can use your slide-notes as a way to jog your memory about things that were said at a specific point in a past lecture. It's quite similar to SoundCloud, which is a hosting service for audio files that lets you leave comments at specific points on a track.

There isn't much more to say about this method; however, I will mention that it's important to remain vigilant about truly learning the material and putting ideas in your own terms. The few times I've used the method in my classes, I found I was much lazier about creating a thorough picture of the material.

Paper Notebooks vs. Laptops

Besides your note-taking system itself, another choice you have to make when taking notes is whether to use plain old paper or a computer. Each method has its benefits and drawbacks.

Taking notes on your computer will typically be much faster than writing them out by hand, and you won't have to deal with hand cramps. Paper, however, is much better for drawing diagrams and pictures - and for math notes, it's the clear winner.

However, what I want to really focus on in this

section is the question of which method is better for **learning**. I came across some interesting research a while back that was published in a journal called *Psychological Science*. Here's the relevant bit:

> *"In the research trial, students who took their notes longhand wrote on average of 173 words compared to computer note takers who wrote 310. Students who typed their notes were also more likely to take down notes word-for-word."*

A lot of students think that they're better off if they record every word that's said in the lecture, and at first this seems logical - if you write down everything, that means you captured it all right?

In reality, though, students who do this actually learn *less* - and here's why. When you're taking notes and a new idea is presented in class, it has to pass through your ears or eyes, and then go through your brain for processing before it ends up in your notes.

When that idea hits your brain, that grey goo up in your skull pays attention to two things:

- **Syntax** - the auditory sounds or printed letters/symbols that make up the message

- **Meaning** - the actual "meat" of the idea, and how it connects to other ideas

Say, for example, that your professor puts up on the board the sentence, "Megatron is a Decepticon." She tells you this because she is awesome and for some reason you're taking an entire class on Transformers.

When each of these words enters your brain, it'll process the symbols that make them up, recognize that they represent certain concepts, and given enough time, connect those concepts to one another as the sentence suggests. Since your brain is a giant, interconnected web of ideas, it'll also connect these concepts to other nodes in the web that were already there.

It'll connect Megatron to the Transformer node, which itself is connected to nodes like "robot", "TV show", and "Shia Labeouf is a terrible actor." (Ok, he wasn't too bad in *Eagle Eye*...)

Decepticon will be connected to the Transformer node as well, but your brain will also connect it to nodes like "group," which itself may be connected to nodes like "reductionism" and "Power Rangers".

Here's the thing: All of this happens when your brain processes the **meaning**. At the same time, part of your brain power is processing the **syntax** of the message so it can direct your hands to write or type it in your notes.

If you devote too much brainpower to processing syntax - that is, if you're trying to record everything in the lecture word-for-word - then there's no brainpower left over for processing meaning. You don't make any of those connections. At this point, you have basically become an unpaid court stenographer.

Going back to the research I cited, the students who typed their notes were much more susceptible to falling into the pattern of copying down lecture material word for word - hence their negatively impacted learning ability.

The lesson here is to be **deliberate** about learning - *especially* if you choose to take your notes on a computer. Since you can type much faster than you write, you have to exercise more vigilance and focus harder on actually learning the material - and leaving out extraneous details that only waste your time.

STEP 3: GET MORE OUT OF YOUR TEXTBOOKS

Reading books is probably one of my favorite things ever, but when reading is assigned… I'm less than enthusiastic about it. Maybe you're the same. Still, a lot of the information you'll need to earn great grades is locked inside required textbooks, so you'll need to read them eventually.

Professors tend to assign *too much* reading, though; you usually don't need to pay super-close attention to everything you're assigned to learn the necessary information to ace your tests.

This chapter will show you how to figure out which reading assignments are actually worth doing, and it'll also guide you through the best strategies for completing those readings quickly and retaining as much important information from them as possible.

Don't Do All Your Assigned Reading

Here's the thing about assigned reading: **you can't do all of it**. And you probably shouldn't.

Most classes assign way too much reading, and for many classes the reading isn't even useful to do for one of two reasons:

- The professor will cover the same material in class, or...
- You won't ever be tested on it

While the material in those textbooks is objectively *useful*, remember the theme of this book - reducing your study time! Your time in college is extremely limited, especially if you're making good use of it by working on projects, building relationships, staying involved in clubs, etc. Oh, and maybe a bit of time to actually relax as well.

Put simply, if your reading assignments aren't absolutely necessary to do, you shouldn't allow yourself the time to do all of them. That time can be better used elsewhere.

But how do you figure out which assignments are necessary, and which ones aren't? The first piece of advice I can give you is this: Readings can be separated into **different categories**:

1. Primary readings
2. Secondary readings

Primary readings generally include the required textbook for the class and possibly other readings based on what you're learning. In general, you should make your best effort to do these readings.

Secondary readings are things like smaller books, articles the professor wants you to read, case studies, etc. In my experience, large portions of my grade never hinged on these types of readings, so they were prime candidates for either quick scanning or skipping altogether.

The other thing I'll say is to constantly **gauge your classes**. Be mindful of how much overlap there is between what's presented in class and what's in the textbook. Pay attention to how much of your exams actually focus on things you could only get from the reading.

By doing this, you'll be able to intelligently adjust your workload to fit your grade goal as the semester goes on without wasting too much time on reading.

Know How You'll Be Assessed

Gauging your classes isn't just useful for figuring out which reading assignments you can skip; it also helps you figure out *how* you should tackle individual reading assignments.

You can gain this insight by focusing on **how you'll be assessed** in a specific class. Different classes will have different types of assessments, including:

- Multiple choice tests
- Essays and written questions
- Data analysis in labs
- Reports and class presentations

The type of assessment you'll be facing should help you define the **specific information** you need to pull out of your readings. You can't remember it all, so the most efficient strategy is to figure out precisely what you need to learn and focus on that.

For example, multiple choice tests require you to learn lots of facts and details from your textbook readings. To account for this, you should make sure you focus on bolded terms, definitions, and any specific details that stick out when you're reading. Your reading notes should reflect this as well, and you should later convert them into rapid-fire questions that you can use to quiz yourself.

On the other hand, essays require you to have a firm grasp of the **main idea** of a reading, and you need to be able to summarize it and build off of it in your own words. To prepare for this, it's better to practice honing in on the *most salient points* of a reading and try to summarize them once you've finished reading.

Don't Read Textbooks Like Newspapers

People generally read newspapers passively, and they do it just to get the gist of the day's events. If you were to ask someone about specific details they'd read in a newspaper the day after they'd read it, you probably wouldn't get good answers in response.

When you read your textbooks, you're reading to **learn** and **apply** the information. You're not just trying to get the gist.

That's why you should do your best to *not* read your textbook like you'd read a newspaper. I call students who do this **textbook zombies** - they're single-mindedly concerned with running their eyes over the assigned pages and then shuffling off to their next planned activity (possibly eating brains?).

Think of your textbook like an art museum. When I went to New York City last summer, I visited the Metropolitan Museum of Art and walked through almost every exhibit.

While I do remember that the Met is the most amazing art museum I've ever been to, I don't really remember the details of the pieces I looked at. That's because I just casually strolled through the halls and looked at the art - I didn't take much time to note down the names of the paintings or who painted them.

Just like passively walking through a museum won't give you a detailed knowledge of the art in it, passively running your eyes over the words in a textbook won't help you really learn the material. And trying to re-read it multiple times won't yield much of an improvement either.

> *"How often you read something is immaterial; how you read it is crucial." - Virginia Voeks*

Instead of reading passively, read as if you were having a conversation with an intelligent friend. When she talks, you listen intently. When she pauses, you contribute your own ideas and, together, you create new information. You come away feeling energized, not drained.

This type of reading is called **active reading**, and it's the key to dealing with your textbooks in the most effective way.

5 Active Reading Strategies

For decades, professors who all belong to the ultra-secret society of Acronym Lords (now that I've told you about it, they're coming for you) have been trying to push active reading systems that can be neatly packaged into - you guessed it - tidy little acronyms.

These systems, like SQ3R (Survey, Question, Read, Recite, Review), SQ4R (add Reflect), and others contain some useful techniques - but I think trying to rigidly follow one every time you read is far too time-consuming. I'm not the only one who thinks this; Cal Newport, the founder of the excellent Study Hacks blog, wrote:

> *"I've never met a high-scoring student who used a system like SQ4R. The reason: they're too time-consuming! What these students do instead is discover simple, streamlined and devastatingly effective heuristics that can be easily adapted to specific classes."*

The only acronym-based reading system I recommend is SCAR:

1. Stop
2. Complaining
3. And
4. Read

So, instead of appeasing the secret acronym society members and recommending a cumbersome system, I'm just going to give you 5 active reading strategies you can adopt as you wish.

Note: Again, including images of each technique would mess up the formatting of the book - but you can see examples in my <u>Active Reading video</u>.

Use the Pseudo-Skimming Technique

The longer a reading assignments is, the more likely a large portion of its paragraphs will be **filler** - stuff you don't really need to read. According to Cal Newport, filler paragraphs can include:

- Background story
- Asides
- Exceptions (because professional scholars want to be thorough)
- Extra details

In many cases, information of these types won't make up the bulk of what you'll be tested over later - so paragraphs containing those types on information should be quickly *scanned*.

However, a good number of paragraphs in any reading will contain **important material** that you should learn. These paragraphs should be read intently.

Enter Cal's **pseudo-skimming** method; essentially, you're going through your readings at a staggered pace. One moment you'll be quickly scanning through paragraphs, the next you'll notice an important paragraph and slow down to take it in fully.

Deliberately attempting to read using the pseudo-skimming method will prevent your brain from automatically giving equal preference to every paragraph in a reading (which, in my case, meant diligently reading each one for the first 10 minutes while my willpower was high, then eventually scanning/skipping as I got further into the chapter and became bored).

Read the Chapter Backwards

Here's the thing about textbook readings... they're usually not suspenseful. They don't have a narrative, and rarely will you spoil yourself by going to the end first.

You can take advantage of this by **reading backwards**. Before you dive into a chapter, flip to the back of it and see what's there. Usually, you'll see a list of key vocab terms, review questions, and other helpful stuff.

Use what you find here to *prime your brain* for the actual reading. Once you've loaded what you can from the review section into the front of your consciousness, you'll be able to pick out those bits more easily when you read them in the actual text.

Create Questions While You Read

One of the concepts I'll be diving deeper into later on in the book is **Active Recall** - the practice of forcing your brain to actually retrieve information instead of just passively exposing yourself to it. Doing this helps you learn much more efficiently.

An easy way to prep for Active Recall-based study sessions is to **create questions** while you do your reading assignments. You should definitely take notes when you read - either during or immediately afterward - and a great way to process these notes for easy studying is to pull details from them and rework them into questions you can quiz yourself on later.

In addition to the details from your notes, another great source of questions is the *section headings* of your actual readings. These generally pull out the main idea of a section, so using them as a basis for a question is a good way to jog your memory of that section's most salient points.

Pay Attention to Formatting

Text in your reading assignments that's **bolded**, *italicized*, or

- sitting nicely
- in lists

…should be given special attention. If text has special formatting, it's a good sign that it represents a main idea, vocab term, or important process that you should learn.

When I took my marketing class, I actually got to the point where I'd just scan through each textbook chapter looking for bolded vocab terms and write them down in my notes. I had figured out that the tests were largely based on these vocab terms along with a few case studies, so I had no need to waste time on all the other details in each chapter of the book.

Mark Up Your Book and Take Notes

Lastly, find a way to make reading a more interactive process by either marking up your books or taking notes on what you're reading. Both of these techniques emphasize active reading over simple, passive exposure, and both will make your later study sessions easier.

If you're renting your textbooks, plan to sell them, or otherwise can't permanently mark them up, you can use sticky flags instead to mark important points in your assignments. These can stick out of your book slightly and give you easy access to places you've marked, even when your book is closed.

If you *can* mark up your books, then you can either use a highlighter or a pencil to make permanent markings. I'm generally not a fan of highlighting; as a sort-of OCD person, I always found myself spending too much time trying to make my highlighted lines nice and straight. For me, using a pencil works so much better.

Not only can you easily underline and bracket important terms, but you can also write short notes in the margins of your book. Remember why Harry Potter's Potions book was so useful in *The Half-Blood Prince?* Margin-notes can really help jog your memory later because they help you connect the reading material to things you already know, making it easier for your brain to solidify your understanding of the topic.

Speaking of notes, one last way to get more interactive with your readings is to take actual notes on them - in a separate notebook or on your computer. This is where **creating questions** can come in handy; you can turn your section headings into questions in your notes, then jot down details from those sections with a goal of answering those questions.

For most books, my preferred method of taking notes is to worry about them *after* I've finished a reading section. I'll typically read a chapter of a book I'm going through once, then open Evernote and create outline-style notes of all the details I remember (I'm trying to use Active Recall during this part to maximize my learning). This is what I'm currently doing as I go through *The Power of Habit* by Charles Duhigg.

Once those details are down, I'll scan through the chapter once more and add anything else I deem important to the notes.

However, when I'm digging through textbooks while trying to find *specific information* - for example, when I'm researching a topic for a new video - I'll have a notebook open while I'm reading and will be jotting down flow-style notes as I go through the book.

Summarize What You Read

I want to put special emphasis on summarizing, as it's about the most useful implementation of an Active Recall strategy you can apply to your reading assignments. When you attempt to summarize what you've read, you're digging into your brain and pulling out the information for, essentially, the task of *teaching* what you read.

You may have heard of the *Learning Pyramid* before:

The Learning Pyramid

Average Retention Rates

5%	Lecture
10%	Reading
20%	Audiovisual
30%	Demonstration
50%	Discussion
75%	Practice
90%	Teach Others

Now, many experts disagree about the accuracy and validity of the learning pyramid, and I wouldn't venture to claim that the percentages listed on it are completely accurate. There are a ton of factors that go into how well you can retain information, not least of which is the actual nature of the information itself - our brains are weird and built upon millions of years of odd, non-logical evolution, so the way they remember facts about math won't be the same they remember facts about the ninja creeping up behind you.

Still, both sense and my own experience tell me that the *bottom* of the pyramid is more or less right -

teaching something results in higher retention in your own brain. This is because you're intensely processing the information with a goal of being able to communicate it in a form that will be understandable to someone less knowledgeable than you.

Summarizing does this really well, so it's a perfect strategy for efficiently learning the most important material from your readings. As I noted above, I tried to summarize what I learned from each chapter in *The Power of Habit* by trying to type out bulleted notes from memory before going back through the chapter and fleshing them out.

You can do this as well, though if the reading you're doing is for a class that'll be assessing you with **essays**, it might be better to try typing out your notes in paragraph form - at least for sections and assignments you deem to be especially important (which means you should definitely be paying close attention to your syllabus and what your professor says).

STEP 4: PLAN LIKE A GENERAL

As a student, your goal should be to never have to say,

> *"Holy banana pancakes, I totally forgot about that assignment."*

College life is a complicated maelstrom of activities, assignments, projects, events, and spontaneous trips to the grocery store at 2 A.M. so you can score free boxes to make cardboard battle armor out of.

Without a good planning system, things **will** fall through the cracks. This chapter is all about helping you form that planning system and build the habits that'll keep it running smoothly.

It's also about helping you be more productive, and here's why…

Planning Mode vs. Robot Mode

As a student, you're not often forced to do specific things at specific times. You have a lot of choice in any given moment.

Jorgen von Strangle, the toughest fairy in the universe, is not standing behind you in preparation to put his boot up your rear every time you have to study. And that's a pity, because it's often *exactly what you need*. Your freedom of **choice** is one of the most devious culprits in the sabotage of your productivity.

Sheena Iyengar, a professor at Columbia Business School, has done a lot of research into the topic of choice. Here's a quote from her that summarizes a lot of her work:

> *"There are times when the presence of more choices can make us choose things that are not good for us. For me, the clearest example is that the more retirement fund options a person has, the less likely they are to save for their old age."*

With a bit of thought, this actually makes quite a bit of sense. A lot of people never start investing because they feel there are *just too many options*, and they're afraid of picking the wrong one. Ironically (and tragically), the most wrong option is usually waiting too long to invest.

As a student, you probably have this problem as well; the only difference is that you're worried about marginal opportunity costs instead of marginal financial returns. You wonder which homework assignment you should tackle first, which class you should study for now and which to save for later, etc.

A successful student doesn't spend very much time on this problem at all because they know how to effectively split their time between their **Planning mode** and their **Doing Mode** (which I like to call Robot Mode instead).

The word "robot" actually comes from the Czech word "robotnik," which directly translates to "worker" or "slave". Workers and slaves do not typically take care of the planning aspects of a projects. However, when motivated properly, they do get down to business and **get stuff done**.

Logically, this means that you want to be in Robot Mode as much as you possibly can during your work sessions. Steps 7 and 8 will go into detail on how to upgrade yourself to be a *better* robot, but in this step we'll talk about how to utilize Planning Mode effectively so you don't have to spend much time in it. In short, the best way to do this is to get your planning done **up front**.

Plan Out Your Entire Education

While most of this chapter is about weekly, in-the-trenches planning, I want to mention the importance of having a plan for your entire education. Doing this really pays off.

As a freshman, I created an Excel spreadsheet that mapped out all the classes I would take over the following eight semesters.

Note: If you'd like, you can <u>download a copy of my spreadsheet</u> for reference.

To do this, I spent a few hours going over all the requirements sheets relevant to my major - the core MIS curriculum, general business requirements, electives and gen. eds, etc. I made sure I knew how many credits I'd need to graduate, how many of those needed to be 300-level or higher, etc.

Then, I created a column for every semester and listed all the classes I would take, being careful to make sure all the requirements for my major were planned for. I also used Excel formulas to create dynamic credit totals, so my sheet would still work if I changed plans later on.

Doing that really came in handy, because I did change plans several times. I ended up changing electives based on new interests I gained, changing the order of certain classes I took, and dropping a program that no longer benefited me.

Each time I changed plans, I always made sure to update the spreadsheet. Doing this ensured that I always knew what my overall graduation plan was. It also kept me mindful of when I could sign up for classes, which I did as early as possible each semester.

Plan Your Week on Sunday

Sunday should be your planning day. You can go ahead and pick another day if you want, but if you do, we totally can't be friends. (Ok, we can - but only if you can beat me in a DDR battle. Which you won't. #comeatmebro)

Seriously though, you should find a day of the week that you use for planning. Sunday is a prime choice, because it's right before you get back into the swing of things for the week.

Luckily, this process shouldn't take you much time. Chapter 6 covers techniques on staying organized and capturing data intelligently, so if you follow the advice there, you'll have an organized planning system that doesn't require much management.

On this planning day, you'll look at your task management system and make a mental note of everything you need to achieve during the week. You'll probably have **academic tasks**:

- Reading assignments
- Homework
- Exam studying
- Group project work

and you'll also have non-academic tasks. Examples:

- Getting your resume reviewed
- Writing a cover letter for a job
- Setting up a meeting with your advisor
- Buying a new notebook from the bookstore
- Filling out your FAFSA
- Hitting the gym (Do you even lift?)

In addition, you'll probably have events with specific start and end times beyond your classes. Job shifts, group meetings, etc. - make sure these are all on your calendar.

Now that you know all that you need to get done during the week, you can move onto the next step of planning - grouping your tasks by **context**.

Understand Task Contexts

When it comes to managing your work, there are only two contexts that you need to concern yourself with:

- High thought-intensity work
- Low thought-intensity work

Work that requires lots of brainpower - reading, research, writing, creative projects, doing heavy math - is of the **high thought-intensity** variety.

Here's the thing about work of this type: It requires long, uninterrupted stretches of focused work to be done properly. If you're trying to write a big research paper in little 20-minute spurts between classes, you're not going to do as good of a job.

When you give highly thought-intense projects the time and attention they deserve, you're much more likely to find yourself in the **flow state** while working on them - that mental state of zen-like focus, where time seems to melt away and you create your best work.

Thinking about your tasks in terms of their contexts

helps you get into that flow state more because you can **batch low-intensity tasks**. By planning ahead, you can block off a few concentrated hours to take care of all these easier tasks - leaving longer time periods open for the focused, high-intensity work that's more valuable to you in the long run.

Another thing to note here: When planning, try to review your past performance at certain times of the day. Do you do your best work in the early morning? Late at night? Right after class ends?

When you know yourself, you can plan for **optimum effectiveness**. If you know you're focused in the early morning, you can choose to schedule your class, work, and social engagements later in the day. You can also take care of your batched low-intensity tasks later on as well, leaving the early mornings open for even more focused work.

Create a Daily Plan

Planning your week out on Sunday (or whatever day you choose) gives you a solid, high-level view of how that week is going to go. It allows you to make sure you're on top of any upcoming events and reduces the chance you'll get blindsided by something.

However, at least in my experience, you can't plan *everything* out on a Sunday. You'll run out of clean pants on Wednesday and realize you need to do laundry the next day. A friend's car will break down in the Target parking lot and they'll need you to come give them a jump. Things will come up unexpectedly, and you'll inevitably realize that there were already tasks lurking in the darkness that you didn't see on Sunday.

That's why I think you should create a **daily plan** as well. You can either do this first thing in the morning, or the night before; either way, it's a good thing to turn into a solid habit. I have my reminder to do so listed in Habitica as part of my morning routine, but in truth, I often sketch it out right before I go to bed at night.

Here's how I create mine; each night, I'll stand in front of the whiteboard in my room. I'll look at my two main time management apps:

- Google Calendar for events and the content I need to create (I keep it planned out there)
- Todoist for individual tasks

Once I've done that, I'll write down a list of tasks on the whiteboard that need to be done the next day.

A lot of productivity experts will tell you that your daily list should have no more than 2–3 tasks on it; otherwise, you're at risk to overwhelm yourself and end up getting nothing done. If I'm being honest, my daily list usually has 6–10 items on it, and the reason for that is because I am a heartless, soulless robot who works pretty much all the time.

...ok, it's not *that* bad - but I do start things at 6 a.m. each day and usually don't finish until 6 p.m. or later, depending on how busy the week is. **However**, I do have a couple of hacks in place to deal with my many, many tasks which you can take advantage of.

Firstly, I try to **prioritize** my daily list by putting the most important tasks at the top of it. On most days, I don't actually finish the whole list, though I do try my damnedest. By putting the most important tasks first, I'm able to get the *best results* possible, even though I'm not reaching 100% list completion.

There's a great analogy I've heard from several different sources that speaks to the wisdom in prioritizing, and it goes something like this. A professor has a giant glass jar in front of him, and surrounding it are four buckets holding four different materials: big rocks, pebbles, sand, and water.

I'll spare you the less relevant part of the story where he does things wrong to bolster the illustration; the ultimate point is that, by putting the big rocks in first and then moving on to the next biggest material, the professor was able to fit all four materials nicely in the jar. When the big rocks are put in first, the gaps they create are easily filled by pebbles, which in turn leave gaps perfect for sand, and so on.

This analogy applies perfectly to the real world; take care of the important things first and you'll get the best results. What's "important?" Think about your tasks in terms of:

- What will get you closest to achieving your goals
- What will prevent your life from spiraling into utter chaos, destruction, and the rise of Beelzebub himself
- What will require the most *willpower* to complete

That third one - willpower - is an especially crucial consideration, as willpower is a finite resource. There are things you can do over the long term to get more, and over the short term to get the most out of your current store, but it *is* limited. Don't waste it on unimportant tasks; as the day wears on, you'll come to find you're unwilling to do the things that actually matter. Remember: **big rocks**.

Secondly, I attempt to estimate the amount of time it'll take to complete each task (accurately - see the section on the Fudge Ratio below). I then add up all the estimates and come up with a total time commitment for the list, which I'll write at the bottom.

Since I typically start my work each day around 8 a.m. after doing my 2-hour morning routine (see the section on that in Step 7), I'll use that total time estimate to come up with an **end goal** for my work day. Doing this helps to *externalize* my motivation to complete my work by creating time pressure that exists outside of my brain. It's not as motivating as a hard deadline (like a due date on a paper), but it helps keep me from working in ultra-long, unfocused stretches.

Try Timeboxing

My time-estimating strategy for my daily plans that I just went over works well for me, but sometimes you want to go a step further. Enter **timeboxing**. This means actually scheduling specific blocks of time for each task on your daily list. Timeboxing is the closest you can get to becoming your own slave-driving asshole of a boss, but it can be effective if you're able to estimate your time blocks well and then stick to the schedule.

I actually tested out timeboxing during a week in the fall. Instead of creating a single-day task list, though, I timeboxed my entire week.

Doing this was the ultimate way of separating Planning Mode and Robot Mode; when I finished planning and started going through the timeboxes, I already had almost *every* choice made for me: I knew exactly what to do, the order in which I needed to do it, and how long each task should take.

You can use timeboxing in multiple ways; in fact, you don't have to apply it to your entire daily plan. Instead, you can simply try using it on one particular project that you know you've been procrastinating on. By setting a timebox, you'll create some time pressure that'll help motivate you to work more quickly.

You can also use timeboxing when you're faced with a project for which you're not feeling a whole lot of clear direction. When you don't know what to do and you're paralyzed because of it, creating a timebox can motivate you to spend that time at least trying to make some progress.

Know Thy Fudge Ratio

Humans are really bad at accurately predicting how long it will take to do things, and this is due to something called the **planning fallacy**. This is a phenomenon in which people's estimates for the time needed to complete a task show optimistic bias. In short, people almost always underestimate the time needed to get something done.

Here's an illustration: In 1995, a Canadian professor of Psychology named Roger Buehler asked his students when they thought they'd be able to complete homework and other tasks. Buehler actually asked for probabilities - specifically, he wanted to know when students thought it was 50%

probable they'd have their projects done, and also when they'd up that to 75% and 99%.

The results?

- 13% finished their work by the time they were 50% sure about
- 19% finished at their 75% probability estimates
- 45% finished before the time they were 99% sure they'd be done at

That last one is the most interesting - *less than half* of the students finished their work in the time they were **99% sure** it would take. They tried to make an extremely conservative estimate, and most were still wrong.

Another psychologist named Ian Newby-Clark discovered the root of the problem in his own studies. He asked research participants for time estimates based on both:

- Realistic, "best guess" cases
- Hopeful, everything-goes-right "best case" scenarios

As it turns out, people's estimates in both cases were virtually identical. The key finding here: When people try to come up with a realistic, "best guess" time estimate, their brains actually consider the **best**

case. We are *very bad* at taking unpredictable setbacks and delays into account when making time estimates.

There's actually a good way of accounting for this problem (unlike many other cognitive biases), and that's to base your prediction on a broad view of the task, rather than all the individual components.

When you do this, you can compare it to similar tasks that have already been completed in the real world, and make your estimate based on the amount of time those tasks actually took. As you do more and more work, you'll have more and more data to pull from when doing this.

However, there's another effective trick you can use in making time estimates called the **Fudge Ratio**. This term was coined by the personal development blogger Steve Pavlina, but it harkens back to a concept thought up by Douglas Hofstadter, the author of what is potentially the most daunting book on my shelf, *Gödel, Escher, Bach: An Eternal Golden Braid*.

Hofstadter's Law, aptly named, states:

> *"It always takes longer than you expect, even when you take into account Hofstadter's Law."*

Hofstadter came up with this law in reference to how long it was taking to develop computers that could become world chess champions (the book was written in 1979), but it applies to a lot of the projects we humans take on.

Pavlina's Fudge Ratio acknowledges the Planning Fallacy and offers up a simple process for fixing it:

1. Write down a list of tasks you need to do.
2. Put an "off-the-cuff" time estimate on each one.
3. As you finish tasks, write down the actual amount of time they took.
4. Divide the actual task time by your estimate to get your Fudge Ratio.

So, for example, say you estimated that it would take you 45 minutes to finish a study guide for your history class. In reality, it takes you 1 hour and 15 minutes. Using math that I learned in 3rd grade when I wasn't thinking about Batman, I can calculate the ratio:

75 minutes/45 minutes = 1.67

Now you know your Fudge Ratio is **1.67** - which means that the next time you need to predict how long it'll take you to finish a similar task, you should multiply your initial prediction by 1.67.

Over time, you won't need to do the math anymore; you just get better at making accurate time estimates. In fact, I *never* did the math. As a student, I started trying to make better predictions before I ever heard about the Fudge Ratio, and the way I did it was to simply try to be **mindful** of how long it took me to get things done. I also tried to predict potential setbacks, distractions, and other things that might derail me from the "best case" scenario.

If you do this, your estimates won't always be perfect - but they'll be a heck of a lot better than the estimates of most other people.

Use the Captain America Method to Break Down Projects

Planning shouldn't stop at the weekly or daily level. Individual projects should be broken into steps and prioritized as well - and your goal here should be to create a list of steps that are **actionable**.

Hypothetical example: "Study for Calculus Final" isn't a good task – it doesn't implicitly tell you exactly what to do, so it should be broken up into action steps that a robot could do, like:

- Set up study area and download practice problem set from Blackboard

- Review chapter on L'Hôpital's rule in textbook and take summarized notes
- Work through problem set

I call this the **Captain America Method**, because I like superheroes and shaky metaphors.

Captain America was able to break a large-scale alien invasion down into components and direct his resources (the Avengers) to each portion; similarly, you should be able to break up your tasks and devote your resources (blocks of time) to each step.

Here's a couple of examples from my own work:

Answering 97 Emails in One Day

I get a lot of email, and I normally try to stay on top of it. Between questions from readers, partnership opportunities, old web design clients, and everything else, I probably get 20–30 emails that **require action** every day.

During the early fall of 2014, I spent quite a bit of time traveling to conferences and other events. As a result, the emails piled up to levels that weren't easy to clear out in a day – so I just neglected them entirely. My negligence eventually culminated in an inbox that held 97 unanswered emails.

Since I delete everything that isn't important every

day, each of these emails that remained in the inbox required some sort of action – essentially leaving me with a 97-item to-do list.

Day after day, I'd tell myself:

"Today the day I'll answer them all!"

I call this the Hulk method, as I was simply trying to **brute force** the task. It didn't work; day after day, I'd try to tackle my inbox, realize how big the task was, and inevitably go do something else.

Then, one day, I decided to draw out a specific plan detailing exactly *how* I'd tackle my emails. I categorized each message, then created steps based on which messages were of the highest priority. Then, I forced myself to go through my inbox in the exact order the steps dictated.

Doing this worked - I finished answering all 97 emails **within 24 hours**. This is the day I came up with the Captain America method, because it was what I was doing: breaking down my task and planning out how I'd devote my resources to it.

Creating Craptons of B-roll

For each of the videos I make for my YouTube channel, I have to create B-roll - all the graphics, animations, and other things that go over the main footage of me talking.

Without B-roll, the videos would be much less interesting. However, creating it is a lot of work. It's a messy process and takes a really long time to do. So, in order to keep my mind focused, I created this list for my video on active reading:

Look at the legend at the top: I've broken this list of 20-something B-roll items down into contexts. Some are just text, some are graphics, and some are full-blown animations.

They're also written in the order that they appear in the video. Lastly, the two columns of checkmarks let me track my progress on both creating the B-roll in Photoshop and including it in my Premiere Pro video project.

With this list in hand, I was able to go down the line on a per-context basis. First, I created almost everything in Photoshop, and then I moved onto Premiere. This was a lot more efficient than switching between the two for each item.

STEP 5: BUILD YOUR OPTIMAL STUDY ENVIRONMENT

Your environment - the area around you, the things that interact with your senses, the systems you interface with to do your work - is hugely influential on your ability to study and work effectively. **Design it deliberately.**

This step will help you optimize your environment in four major ways:

- Finding the best study location
- Selecting great study music/noise
- Limiting real-world distractions
- Limiting technological distractions

Let's get into it.

Location

For me, one of the most important aspects of a study location is the *vibe*. By that, I mean:

> *"What are the other people around me doing?"*

If the people around me are working diligently, then I feel more motivated to work - in fact, it almost feels like an obligation at that point. I'd almost feel like I'm bringing down the collective productivity of the room if I slacked off.

For that reason, I'm a huge fan of studying and working at libraries, coffee shops, and co-working places. I actually took this to the extreme during my senior year; I had taken on an independent study class (my method of weaseling out of a required class I didn't want to take), and my project was to build an iPhone app.

The only problem was… I didn't know how to do it. Between my other classes and projects, I also was having a lot of trouble finding the motivation to crack open the iOS programming book I'd bought. So, I decided to go **nuclear**.

It was about a month into the semester when my friend Alex told me about a new conference going on in Austin, Texas called FU Weekend. The entire point of the conference was to get a bunch of people together who all had creative projects that just weren't getting finished - and to **finish them**. There was an application process, and the organizers were selective in order to keep the conference limited to people who would actually show up and do work.

I applied and got accepted about a week before the conference started. To get there, I had to drop $600 on a plane ticket to Austin *and* skip an exam that I hadn't known was on the same day as the conference (I got to make it up, fortunately).

That's a lot of money and effort just to finish a school project - *but it paid off*. I ended up meeting a ton of awesome people over that weekend, including one of the people who works at Treehouse - an amazing learning library similar to Lynda.com. He pointed me to their iOS course, which turned out to be much easier for me to follow than the book.

Over the course of just two days, I learned the basics of iPhone programming and built **two apps**. I got 95% of the work for the entire independent study project done in that weekend, and I attribute that to the fact that I was surrounded by a group of insanely motivated people who were all working hard on their own projects. There was a feeling that great things were being created there, and I wanted my weekend to have a great output as well.

Another thing to take into account with your choice of location is the specific tasks you have on your plate - and what tools you need for them. If you need to write a huge research paper, for example, the library is a great choice because you're surrounded by research materials you may need.

Your environment can reduce the *friction* involved in getting into your work by giving you easy access to tools and resources you may need. Think about this factor when selecting your study spot.

Study Music

Listening to music while studying is one of those little things that people like to argue about. Some people think it hurts your concentration, some think it helps.

For me, it definitely helps. So all I'm going to say about this before recommending some great music sources is to **experiment**. Figure out what works for you, take steps to know yourself, and study better going forward.

Also the whole music vs. no music debate is pretty black and white on the surface, as there are a ton of different varieties of music and "music" you can study with:

1. Music with vocals
2. Purely instrumental music
3. Ambient noise
4. White noise (or pink/brown noise)

The type of music I prefer depends on the type of work I'm doing. If I'm going through a process, such as creating graphics for a post (something I've done countless times), I can listen to anything. It might be metalcore, it might be rap, or it might be weird remixes of anime theme songs. Basically, whatever boosts my energy levels is good. This goes for purely logical tasks as well, such as programming. Even if I'm writing code I haven't had to write before, I can put on any kind of music and be fine.

When it comes to writing, reading, or studying, it's a different story. At that point, I need music that's 99% instrumental, and it needs to be somewhat calm. I can recommend several artists if you're looking to expand your selections:

- 65daysofstatic - electronic-influenced post-rock
- Jordan Tice - instrumental bluegrass
- Pretty Lights - chill electronic
- Balmorhea - post-rock

...and if I don't stop myself, I could probably fill another book with recommendations (I like curating music).

Actually, a lot of my favorite study music picks are individual tracks off of albums that wouldn't otherwise be fit for studying; for example, many metal bands have one or two instrumental tracks or interludes in the middle of their albums.

Additionally, you'll find plenty of great study music in the soundtracks of movies, video games, and anime. There's also a thriving online community for a PC game called Touhou, and within it you'll find hundreds of fan-made songs - many of which are piano-only or otherwise fit for studying.

If you're looking for a good place to find great new study music, I've been working on a YouTube playlist for the last year called <u>The Ultimate Study Music Playlist</u>. As of this writing, it's got 151 songs of all different genres. I always put it on when I need to read or write something (I'm listening to it right now, actually).

While you're at it, you may want to subscribe <u>to my YouTube channel</u> as well. If the content in this book is helpful to you, you'll find a lot more there. I release new videos every week.

So what if you don't work well with music at all? Well, you can study in absolute silence - or you can try out a couple of other options.

The first alternative is **white noise**, which I would

describe as the sound of static, or possibly of a fan blowing. It's constant, unobtrusive, and a lot of people like it better. You can also opt for pink noise or brown noise, both of which emphasize lower frequencies than white noise. Pink noise is a good middle ground. Here are a few places where you can get good white noise:

- SimplyNoise - simple; offers white, pink, and brown noise
- White Noise & Co - gives you a much more customizable spectrum to play with
- Celestial White Noise - this is a 10-hour YouTube video with a unique, "spacey" white noise that I like better than the others
- Space Odyssey - another 10-hour YouTube video; this one's a bit more subdued.

Lastly, there's **ambient noise**. This is basically noise you'd hear in specific environments, such as coffee shops, or during events like thunderstorms. I actually *much* prefer ambient noise to both white noise and silence, and have a few different resources for it that you can check out:

- Coffeetivity - coffee shop din (multiple choices)
- RainyMood - rain
- SoundSleeping - lots of different environmental sounds, and you can mix them!

- <u>Ravenclaw Common Room</u> – this site actually has tons of ambient soundscapes, but I
  just had to highlight this one.
- *Bonus:* Actually go to a place with ambient
  noise

Protip: Try mixing some of the ambient sounds with
music from the study playlist! Personally, I like
mixing RainyMood or Coffeetivity with my music.

Limiting Real-World Distractions

Back in Step 4, I mentioned something called the flow
state - a state of mind where you're perfectly focused
on the task at hand. When you're in the flow state,
time seems to slip by, your mind is attuned to its job,
and things seems to get done with ease. It's total
immersion in what you've set your mind to.

When you study or work on a project, you want to
find your way to the flow state. It won't always
happen, but you want to get into it as much as you
possibly can. For that reason, **distractions** are your
worst enemy when you're trying to study. They pull
you right out of the flow state, break your
concentration, and impede your progress.

So how do you limit your exposure to distractions
and also increase your ability to ignore the ones that
do crop up? Let's start with the first one - how to
avoid them as much as possible.

As I mentioned earlier, your choice of study location **really** matters for avoiding distractions. It may actually be the most important thing. I mean, think about it: how much studying could you get done about the Mongol invasion of China if you were *actually at* the Mongol invasion of China? Probably none, because a crazed Mongol would stand on his horse and shoot you in the face with an arrow. Boom, I'm a genius.

Even if you didn't happen to get the one time machine off eBay that actually works, you're still going to need to be discerning about location. Studying in your dorm while your roommates play Guitar Hero is probably not going to go as well as if you chose the library. So be selective about your study location - but also remember that it's still largely personal, so don't think that one person's be-all, end-all mantra of, "Library or nothing!" needs to be the rule for you as well.

Another huge source of distraction is **people** - both those who are working on the same task as you, and those who just happen by. When my friends and I would try to get together in the dorm's shared den and study, we usually would end up messing around with Duke Nukem sound boards and throwing things at each other.

Studying with my friends was a bad idea; getting together with some people from my class, however, was much better. I got a lot done that way.

People who just "happen by" are also bad news bears for your productivity. Assuming you get a job with a cubicle after graduation, you'll probably have to deal with the annoying coworker who saunters by your cubicle to make small talk about his kid's pee wee football game last night while you're simultaneously trying to finish a huge project for the boss and will your brain to just leave this cruel world so it won't have to hear about his kids anymore.

These people don't magically become distraction machines when they get jobs; oh no, they are meticulously honing their skills in college. And college is a much more fertile ground for digging up tantalizing distractions. They will find you in the library and let you know they're going out for pizza, then seeing that movie you've *really* been wanting to see right after.

> *"Oh, you've got a Calc final tomorrow morning? Eh, you'll do fine, bro - don't worry about it!"*

Honestly, the best thing you can do in this situation is to:

- Build up a strong tolerance for saying no to fun things

- Make it difficult for them to contact you

You can close your door or find a secret study spot to avoid them physically, but you've also got electronic communication to worry about. I'll deal with that in the next section, along with other technology-based distractions.

Limiting Technology-Based Distractions

When it comes to technology, probably the worst distraction you face is the vastness of the internet. The best way to prevent yourself from wasting time online is to block your access to the places where you waste it. Plain and simple.

While blocking specific sites won't prevent you from finding new ones to waste time at, it's still effective. The idea is to make procrastination more effort than it's worth.

If your brain is used to jetting over to Reddit or Facebook when you don't want to work, block those two sites. It'll take more mental effort to Google for something specific to waste time looking at than it will for you to just lazily scroll through your news feed.

Here are some apps you can use to block familiar time-wasting sites when you're working:

- <u>StayFocusd</u> (Chrome extension) – this is what I use personally
- <u>FocalFilter</u> (Windows) – blocks access in all browsers
- <u>ColdTurkey</u> (Windows) – like FocalFilter, but can block other programs too. Paid, but you set the price and proceeds go to charity.
- <u>SelfControl</u> (Mac) – same as FocalFilter

If you don't want to use an app, you can also permanently block websites by editing the HOSTS file on Windows or etc/hosts on OS X.

To get really nuclear, make these changes on an Administrator account on your computer. Set a really complex password for that account, and store it somewhere safe on paper.

Do all your work on a non-admin account, and you'll have no way to change your block settings unless you go get the password. This is way more intense than most people will need, but desperate times sometimes call for desperate measures.

If you're one of those students with more than one computer (as an IT major, I always was), you can further remove the temptation to waste time by dedicating one of your computers solely to work.

Don't install stuff like Steam, social media clients, or chat clients (unless they're work-related). You can use the blocking techniques above to completely lock the computer down if needed as well.

If you use Chrome and have Chrome sync enabled for your account, consider using a different Google account on this computer so your time-wasting bookmarks don't sync over. If you don't want to do that, at least hide the bookmarks bar.

It's even more effective if you use this computer in a different location than where you use your leisure computer.

Find a specific spot on campus, in a coffee shop, or somewhere else you like and think of it as your "office". Or pick new locations whenever you like – but don't use the same room you game in.

Don't have a second computer? You don't need to go buy a new one just to use this technique. Just use computer labs on campus to do your work.

I actually did this quite often in school, and the lack of access to all of my time-wasting programs and bookmarks really helped me. It's hard to slack off when you're using a computer with nothing but IE (blegh) and Word, especially if you left your phone back in your dorm.

Now, even if you've gone to nuclear lengths to keep yourself away from distracting websites, you've still got other people to deal with. If your friends are messaging you constantly, you're not going to be able to get much done. So make sure you've signed out of Facebook, gChat, and other messaging services while you're studying.

In order to stay contactable, you can study with Pomodoros and allow yourself to check messages during the short breaks between each one.

Lastly, your **phone** can be a huge distraction while you're studying - *especially* if you've got a lot of notifications coming in all the time. When your phone buzzes with a notification, it triggers a habit to check it. For most people, that habit is really hard to avoid carrying out.

Avoid the trigger entirely by turning off most notifications on your phone. Seriously, you don't need to be notified whenever you get an email or Facebook message - you can easily check those later on.

Another thing you might try doing is putting your phone on Do Not Disturb mode. On the iPhone, this mode prevents calls, texts, and notifications from making any noise. I often use it when I really need to focus.

STEP 6: FIGHT ENTROPY AND STAY ORGANIZED

An organized student is an efficient student, right? Well, most likely, anyways.

Keeping your systems well-organized and free of clutter won't guarantee that you'll study diligently and get your work done, but it'll certainly make it easier to do so.

This step will give you systems for processing computer files, organizing anything you write, quickly capturing data and doing useful things with it when you're on the go.

In addition, it'll also help you to keep these systems in working order as the semester wears on.

Organize Your Files the Right Way

Nothing sucks more than frantically searching through your European vacation pictures folder for *EnglishPaperFinalVersion6-ActuallyFinalThisTime.docx* right before it's due, only to realize a moment too late that you lazily put it in your Borderlands 2 game saves folder instead.

That's why you need to learn how to organize your files properly. I committed to doing this when I started college, and as a result…

- I've never lost an important file since starting college
- I've never been in a situation where I didn't have access to an important file (thanks to Dropbox)
- It takes me almost no time at all to locate any file I need

Contrast this to my high school experience, in which I lost several flash drives and had probably the most convoluted and unorganized computer ever (it didn't help that I shared it with my brother).

The benefits come at a small price, though. Firstly, you have to take the time to properly set up your file system.

This might take longer if you've already got a ton of

files, but it's worth it in the end.

Once your system's set up, you've got to make sure you save your files in the right place, and you've also got to stop yourself from creating new folders in the wrong places. Yeah, it's a bit of work, but again, it's worth it.

First and foremost, download and install Dropbox. You've probably heard of Dropbox before, but I'll refresh your memory about its features real quick:

- Dropbox creates a folder on each computer you've installed it on
- Files in this folder are synced to the cloud and kept updated on all your computers
- All your files are also available to download from your profile on the Dropbox website, and from their mobile apps
- You get 2gb of storage for free - more than enough for most types of schoolwork

The upshot of all this is that you'll always have access to your files wherever you are, as long as you've got a computer with an internet connection (or your smartphone), and you know your Dropbox login info.

You can also use Google Drive, which actually gives you more space (15gb) for free. I've used Dropbox for years and love it, so that's why it's my base recommendation, but Drive is a good option as well.

Next, you need to set up your **folder structure**.

On each of my computers, I put my Dropbox folder in a pretty high level place, like my Documents folder. It doesn't really matter, but since it forms the foundation of my file system, it feels better to have it there.

From there, I break my life down into components and create folders for each of them. The photo below shows several levels of my Dropbox. The main folder has folders for college, this blog, my freelance web design, learning projects, etc.

I've also got a place for folders I share with others, as well as a folder for Notepad++ portable, just in case I find myself using a random computer and need access to a better text editor.

The main thing you should pay attention to here is my "College" folder, which I've drilled into a bit more so you can see how it's organized. My method to organizing the madness that is college goes like this:

- School year (I moved my Freshman folder to long-term storage to save space at one point)
- Class (all non-project files for each class go here)
- Specific project folders

I've also got a Clubs folder for things pertaining to clubs and organizations, as well as an Admissions folder that holds copies of admissions documents and the like.

Once you've got a structure like this, you simply have to keep it organized, save things in the right place, and be disciplined enough not to deviate from it when creating new folders. Organization FTW!

Build a Quick Capture System

David Allen – author of *Getting Things Done* and probably the most well-known productivity nerd alive – aptly describes the purpose of your mind:

> *"Your mind is for having ideas, not holding them."*

In this case, I define the concept of an idea somewhat

broadly: An idea is anything that might cause you to take action at some point in time. This means an idea could be:

- An actual, creative idea you come up with
- An article or book you find that you'd like to read
- A task that needs doing later
- An event you need to attend
- A person you'd like to get to know

Most of these things are not ideas themselves, but your mind holds ideas of them – and that's the problem. Even though your brain is essentially a giant parallel processor that can do many things at once, it generally works best if you've got it pointed at a single task at a time. Trying to juggle a bunch of ideas which require future action only hampers your ability to execute on the idea you're trying to work on now.

But here's the problem: **Ideas come all the time.** Since ideas can strike at any time or place, you need a system for capturing them, storing them away safely for later use, and getting yourself back on task. What's more, you need a system that lets you do this *quickly* and without much friction. This is the idea behind **quick capture.**

To utilize this concept well, you need to build a great quick capture system. The classic method is carrying around a notebook wherever you go, and it's a fine method. I recommend trying it if you like writing with pen and paper.

However, I get a bit geekier with my system, and most of it resides on my iPhone. Here are the apps I use, along with Android alternatives if needed:

- **Drafts** (iOS) - an app that instantly opens to a blinking cursor so you can just *write.* It's the fastest way to enter text on my phone. It's also got smart shortcuts to actions I can take after writing - I generally sent my notes to Evernote for later processing. *Android alternative:* Evernote (there's nothing like Drafts that I've found, unfortunately)
- **Scanbot** (iOS/Android) - a document scanner app. I generally use it for scanning receipts for my business, but it's amazing for scanning handwritten notes as well.
- **Trello** (iOS/Android) - an amazing project management app (more about it in Step 10). If I get ideas on a project I've already planned out, I often add them here.
- **Google Calendar** (iOS/Android) – my favorite calendar app; I've been using this since high school and it's still an integral part of my system today.
- **Todoist** (iOS/Android) - tasks I need to do later get entered here. This is my to-do app of choice.

Lastly, I use <u>Pinboard</u> to keep a well-tagged collection of web pages I want to save for later.

Get a Second Brain

For almost six years now, I've been operating at a significant advantage to most other people on Earth. Why? **I've got two brains.** Ok, maybe it's not all that crazy - but I do have a tool that I refer to as my "second brain," and it's called <u>Evernote</u>.

Evernote is, at a glance, a simple note-taking app. However, there are reasons it became my *most-used application* throughout my entire college career, as well as in my career as a writer/podcast/video producer/beard model today. I used Evernote to take detailed, Outline-style notes in most of my classes throughout college, and it also held group meeting notes, project details, and lots of other things that pertained to school.

In addition, Evernote is where almost every piece of College Info Geek gets its start. I have notebooks in it for:

- Articles, podcast notes, and video ideas
- Large guides and book outlines (this book started as an outline in Evernote)
- Speaking notes and resources
- Testimonials and reader questions

- Various notes from website changes and other technical stuff

Evernote also runs much of my personal life as well. I have personal notebooks for:

- Life details - apartment info, ISP information, account numbers for utilities and other random things
- Software licenses and support contact information
- Rap lyrics
- Magic: The Gathering decks and combo ideas
- Fiction that never sees the light of day
- Travel info - all flight/hostel confirmations, info about where I'm going, conference registrations
- Dance Dance Revolution goal progress (I'm trying to beat every song on Doubles mode)

Lastly, I have a notebook dedicated to **book notes.** Every day, I have a habit of reading for 15 minutes and taking detailed, summarized notes of what I learned. This helps me retain *much* more of the important material in each book I tackle.

Like Dropbox, Evernote syncs all your notes to the cloud. You can access them via any of their desktop or mobile apps, and also via the web app. Also, Evernote can capture notes in formats besides text -

you can record voice notes, and when you capture picture notes, Evernote will even **make any text in the images searchable.** That's right - you can take a picture of a syllabus with your phone, then search for details in the text later. It's amazing.

When I was a student, I was able to pull up my notes right on my phone while waiting for exams so I could quickly review. Evernote has also saved my butt on more than a few occasions; getting into the habit of saving anything I think I might need later in it has really paid off.

If you're going to take lecture notes on a computer, I highly recommend doing it in Evernote. Even if you take them on paper, you can choose to photograph them and import them into Evernote notebooks later if you'd like to make them searchable or accessible from anywhere.

Use a Task Manager

In Step 4, I talked about how you should plan your week out on Sundays. Well, there's a prerequisite to being able to do that effectively - and that's to make sure you have a system that captures tasks you need to complete.

You probably already knew this, so at this point you're asking:

"What's the best to-do app out there?"

I'm gonna make like a smarmy politician and give you an answer that sort of dodges the question: **The best to-do app is the one that works well for you.**

Dodgy, yes... *but it's true.* I went through four years of college constantly reading app review blogs, looking for the absolute best task manager. I figured there must be one to rule them all. What I've learned now, though, is that we're all a bunch of weirdos with non-robotic brains that work in funny ways.

Some people might find a simple notebook works best for them. Others may want to stick to paper, but need more organization a la a system like Bullet Journal. Some are like me and want to use a computer-based system, but then are faced with so many choices:

- Wunderlist
- Remember the Milk
- Google Tasks
- Todoist
- Producteev
- Omnifocus
- Asana

...the list goes on and on. My suggestion would be to try a few out and see what works best for you. Maybe even try a few unconventional ones - I've seen people turn Trello (a project management app) into individual daily task managers. Some people find the simple to-do column in Habitica works well (it's not enough for me though).

The one thing you *must* do, however, is actually **use one.** Don't think you can get by just trying to remember everything you need to do; stuff will inevitably fall through the cracks. Remember, your brain is for *having* ideas, not holding them.

So, given that I've acknowledged the individual nature of task management, the app that *my* weirdo brain currently likes best is called **Todoist.** It's got a nice, clean design, offers apps for both Windows and OS X along with every major smartphone platform, and has a great web app to boot.

Todoist's sparse, minimalist design attracts me in a way that Wunderlist's wooden theming doesn't, though the two apps are very similar in terms of features. One thing Todoist does have that Wunderlist doesn't, though, is *Labels.* Both apps allow you to create multiple lists, which is great for segmenting your life into sensible parts (School, Work, Homework, Clubs), but Todoist's labelling feature also allows me to assign **contexts** to my tasks.

As I talked about in Step 4, it's good to think about your tasks in terms of contexts like *high mental intensity* and *low mental intensity*. The labeling system in Todoist allows me to assign these contexts in real life, and the app has smart text recognition that lets me do it very quickly. For example, entering:

Reschedule meeting with Barrett @low

…will add that task and let me sort it with all my low-intensity tasks. I also have friends that create other types of contexts, such as "social" to group it with all tasks that involve other people, "public" for all that involve leaving the house, etc.

Fight Entropy

Entropy is defined as a general decline into disorder. This is (probabilistically) how the universe works, which is why we have the Second Law of Thermodynamics: **Entropy always increases.**

It's also how organization works for most students. You start the semester out with a well-oiled system of organization. Your files are in their rightful place. You've got neat folders in your backpack, each with an uncrumpled syllabus tucked into it. Your to-do list is well-pruned.

A couple months later, everything is in disarray. The backpack is a mess, you've lost several papers, and your to-do list is full of a bunch of old tasks that gunk it up and obscure the important ones that *need* to be done.

This "entropy" increases friction, makes it harder for you to see what needs to be done, and generally slows you down. Trying to work within messy, high-entropy systems is the equivalent to trying to run through a field of waist-high molasses.

That's why you must **fight the entropy.** Use your Sunday planning sessions not only to create an overall plan for the week, but to keep your task management and file organization systems well-organized. Run through a regular checklist:

- If you've saved files to your desktop in a hurry, move them to where they belong
- Organize Evernote documents if you've sent raw ones from Drafts or entered them hurriedly into a default notebook
- Finish, delete, or re-schedule tasks that are left in your task management system
- Keep your backpack and room organized

Remember, having to deal with friction will reduce your motivation to study, especially as the semester wears on and life gets generally more complex. Constant vigilance!

STEP 7: DEFEAT PROCRASTINATION

I... procrastinated on this chapter. It's actually one of the last chapters I wrote for this book, even though the topic is one I'm quite knowledgeable and passionate about.

Why? Oh, **perfectionism** mostly - since I've done a lot of work on procrastination (blog posts, podcasts, videos, coaching), I felt like this chapter needed to be the most well-written, smooth, info-packed one in the book.

So I left it sitting while I wrote the rest of chapters in relative perfectionism-less bliss. Now, this is some-what ok, as I have a 500 word/day writing habit that ensured the chapter would get done eventually... but without that habit, I might have waited months to write this.

If you're anything like me, **procrastination** - caused by perfectionism or any other reason - is a major stressor in your life. Heck, maybe this chapter alone is the main reason you bought this book.

Since I started College Info Geek, I've done a *lot* of research on procrastination. At this point, I could probably write an entire book about it - and it's actually my intention to do so (one of my main goals is to write a traditionally published book on productivity).

However, this book is about earning awesome grades - and beating procrastination is just one small part of that. So you only get a chapter right now. Still, it's a pretty important chapter, and we've got quite a few bases to cover in our journey to turning you into a focused, task-crunching machine.

Get Over "I Don't Feel Like It."

The #1 reason people procrastinate is this simple string of five words:

"I don't feel like it."

I hear people say this every. Single. Day. I hear it

from multiple people, and some of them say it over and over. I even say it myself.

It's the easiest excuse in the book. Don't feel like doing something? Eh, it's probably not going to kill you if you wait on it. You can always go to the gym tomorrow. That book you're reading isn't going to burst into flames if you don't read a chapter tonight.

Embrace the Netflix…

Here's the thing, though….

Saying, "I don't feel like it," does ABSOLUTELY NOTHING to limit your choices going forward.

That may be the most important sentence in this entire book. Burn it into your brain.

There is no invisible Ghost of Not Feeling Like It that forces your mouse to click on your Reddit bookmark instead of your study guide. Neither does it paralyze you and prevent you from going on a run.

While it's true that every action we take as humans requires some amount of motivation, the grand majority of us have enough willpower to do the things we've committed ourselves to doing. We have enough stored up to get over, "I don't feel like it," though it might take a bit of effort to muster it.

You dug holes in the sandbox as a kid, right? (Or am I just weird?) Scooping up the sand was really easy. Once you hit the dirt, digging became a little bit harder, but it was still doable. After that, you'd hit clay and the work became pretty tough. You had to really press that little plastic shovel hard to dig up the clay.

Eventually, you'd hit rock and wouldn't be able to dig anymore. But, with effort, you were at least able to get past the dirt and clay to reach that point.

Your willpower reserves are the same. There's a small "sand layer" of willpower that you get each day. After you've used that up, you still have a considerable amount left - it just takes some effort to tap into it.

To tap that willpower and get over "I don't feel like it," I've modified my vocabulary a bit. Now, I never say those five words alone anymore; instead, I say,

> *"I don't feel like it - but I'm going to do it anyway."*

Embracing this mindset and actually putting it into action afterwards takes **grit** - a willingness to be uncomfortable. For most of us, life is ridiculously comfortable, which makes it tempting to avoid things that are hard and to stay comfortable.

Building up a tolerance to uncomfortable situations will help you get over a lack of easily tappable willpower. I actually take ice cold showers every day in order to build my own grit; it's a deliberate choice to be uncomfortable that I make daily.

Understand the Procrastination Equation

Can you actually quantify your motivation levels? According to **Temporal Motivation Theory,** you can. Developed by motivation researcher Piers Steel, this theory posits an actual equation with several factors that can be used to explain motivation.

This is called the **Procrastination Equation,** and it can be a useful tool for pinpointing exactly *why* you might be feeling a lack of motivation to get something done. Here's the equation:

$$Motivation = \frac{Expectancy \cdot Value}{Impulsiveness \cdot Delay}$$

On the left side, we've got the end value **Motivation,** the resource you use to complete any task for which you expect a particular reward.

Now let's break down each of the components on the right side:

- **Expectancy:** Your perceived odds of being able to complete the task and get the reward. How confident are you that you can succeed?
- **Value:** How valuable the task's reward is to you. Do you really care about what you'll get when you finish?
- **Impulsiveness:** How likely you are to get sidetracked. For me, this could be rewritten as: How close am I to people who are playing Smash Bros?
- **Delay:** The time it'll take to achieve the task and get the reward. This may be defined by a hard deadline/due date, or it may be defined simply by how long it'll likely take you to do the work required.

In most cases, you won't be able to do much about Delay. For example, if you're working on a term paper, the deadline is pretty much fixed. You've got to turn it in on time or you fail.

The other components, though, are more malleable. Therefore, if you're experiencing a lack of motivation, you need to do one of three things:

- **Increase your expectancy** - do something that increases your confidence in being able to complete the task.

- **Increase the task's value** - make the reward greater, or tweak the process of doing the work in order to make it more enjoyable.
- **Decrease your impulsiveness** - figure out how to avoid distractions, remain focused, and work diligently.

Luke Muehlhauser, a writer I've been following for some time, <u>outlined an **algorithm** of sorts</u> that he follows when he finds himself procrastinating. Here it is:

- *Notice* you're procrastinating. Deliberately state it to yourself, "I am procrastinating right now."
- Try to guess *which* part of the equation is causing you trouble. Are you feeling impulsive? Does the reward not motivate you? Are you not feeling up to the task?
- Find a way to *fix* that problem area.

If the Value is low, you could gamify the task or add an additional, fun reward to its completion. If you're experiencing low Expectancy, try breaking down the task further so you can complete part of it and start building some confidence-boosting success spirals.

For the problem of Impulsiveness, try the environment design techniques in Step 5 and set time-based goals.

Build Strong Habits

The science of willpower is a detailed, complicated field. However, there's really only one thing you need to know about it right now: **Willpower is a limited resource.** Whenever you have to motivate yourself to do something, you're pulling from a finite source of willpower.

However, your *habits* don't need to pull from willpower. Habits govern far more of your behaviors than you might think, and the good thing is that you can create new, positive habits with some up-front effort. Once you've encoded a task as a habit, you'll be able to complete it on a regular basis without having to use up a ton of willpower.

This is good, because one of the true keys to success in college is putting in **consistent, daily effort.** Your workload is almost always large, and the best way to stay on top of it, keep your stress levels low, and maximize your learning potential is to make sure you're putting in effort every single day.

When you turn this daily effort into a habit, great results will follow. Here's some proof:

- By designing a habit to write 500 words a day, I was able to finish most of this book in a couple months' time.

- A habit of reading and taking notes has resulted in a *Book Notes* folder in Evernote with over 7,000 words of notes on three different books over the past month.
- Doing four sets of 10 pull-ups every day has increased my max number of pull-ups in one set to 17 (when I started I could only do 6).

Deliberately designing habits and making sure to stick to them until they become natural has had incredible effects upon my health, learning, and business. In fact, since becoming serious about my habits, the number of visitors to my website has gone up over 200%; I've been able to publish more than double the number of posts that I used to; and my daily energy levels have increased as well.

So how do you start building strong habits? My suggestion is to use **Habitica.** This is a website that helps you build habits by using video game elements, specifically those taken from RPGs like Final Fantasy and Dragon Warrior.

By completing daily habits and tasks, your character in Habitica will gain experience and gold, which will let you level up and buy items respectively. You can also join **Parties** with other players, and this is where Habitica becomes *really* effective. If you start a quest with your party members and fail to do your daily habits, you'll take damage - **but so will your party members.** In order to keep them from getting pissed at you, you'll need to make sure you complete your habits every day.

I've been questing with four College Info Geek readers for a couple months now, and during that time I've not even *thought* about skipping my daily habits. It wouldn't be fair to them. Plus, since I've been tracking my habits in Habitica for so long, most of them are just natural now.

Lastly, you can join interest-based **Guilds** in Habitica, which let you chat with other players and take part in challenges. And guess what? Yep, you guessed it - there's a <u>College Info Geek guild</u> available to join.

As of this writing, we've got around **7,500** members. I'd love for you to join in, jump in the chat room, and help build everyone's motivation levels. We also have monthly challenges you can join in order to build your skills in real life.

Avoid Low-Density Fun

I have friends who almost never let themselves do the really fun things they want to do during the semester. They'll talk about how much they want to play a certain game or watch a new movie, but when I suggest that they just go play it, they'll say:

"I really can't; I have way too much homework and I'd feel guilty."

Five minutes later, though, I'll see them scrolling through their Facebook feed.

This is a common problem, and I call it the problem of **low-density fun.** Scrolling through your news feed or watching a few funny videos on YouTube is easy, and it's sort of fun to do. However, because it's so easy and feels so unlike "real" fun, it's easy to not feel guilty about it - which leads to a lot of procrastination.

Sadly, if these friends could just avoid the low-density fun, they'd get their work done faster and actually have time for those medium/high-density fun things they wanted to do in the first place.

The solution? **Commit to having your high-density fun.** If you want to play *Skyrim* later, commit to starting it at 8 p.m. Then, make sure all your work is done by then. Let your high-density fun create a deadline that propels you into focused work.

Combined with the distraction-fighting techniques in Step 5, this can be a really effective way of overcoming procrastination.

Use the Pomodoro Technique

The Pomodoro Technique is a simple way to get yourself started on a task when you just can't seem to focus. The method is named after a "pomodoro" (tomato-shaped) kitchen timer, which is the tool that was traditionally used for it.

To use this technique, follow these steps:

- Commit to focusing on **one** task
- Set a timer for 25 minutes
- During that time, do as much work as you can on the task. Don't let yourself do anything else.
- After the timer rings, give yourself a short break (3-5 minutes)

Once you've completed a session, write down what you accomplished during it. Keep doing this during all the Pomodoro sessions you're able to do while studying.

A key part of this technique is the postponing of interruptions; if you're distracted during a session by something, you should quickly pause and schedule some time in the future to take care of that distraction - then get back to work.

The idea behind the Pomodoro Technique is to create as much "flow" time as possible. By deliberately postponing any distractions (that can't be ignored altogether), you encourage your brain to spend more time in that flow state.

When All Else Fails, Bring the Pain

There's a blogger I follow named Maneesh Sethi who actually hired a girl off of Craigslist to sit next to him in a coffee shop and *slap him in the face* whenever he started procrastinating. Now, he's developing a wearable device that will deliver an electric shock when you aren't doing what you're supposed to be doing.

These things might sound crazy, but it's undeniable that pain can be a motivating factor. If the result of *not* doing a task is much less pleasant than actually doing it, we'll always do it.

If you're really struggling with procrastination, you can try to use this to your advantage. You don't necessarily need to use physical pain, either - a threat of loss or embarrassment can work just as well.

For example, I use a website called Beeminder to put a little bit of a threat on my blog's publishing schedule. Beeminder lets you set goals and actually pledge money towards them; if you fail to stick with your goal, the site will charge you whatever you pledged.

105

I have a <u>goal in Beeminder</u> to publish 3 pieces of content every week; currently, if I fail, I'll lose $10. Every time you fail, however, the price to recommit triples. They also have a premium feature that lets you set a custom pledge amount - the writer Nick Winter pledged over **$7,000** in order to force himself to write a book.

You can use Beeminder to track almost any kind of goal, and there are other ways you can introduce a threat into your goals as well. You could get an accountability partner, for example. I really liked <u>this guy's</u> hilarious deal with his roommate:

> *Back when I was in college, my roommate and I had a pact.*
>
> *During finals week, if one of us caught the other slacking off and not studying, we were obligated to destroy something of theirs.*
>
> *The pact ended after I found him playing Madden and cut his shoe in half with a kitchen knife.*
>
> *I guess he wasn't taking it as seriously as I was.*

Adding threats to your goals is a bit of a nuclear option, but it can be effective!

STEP 8: STUDY SMARTER

Much of this book has already tackled topics that can help you become better at studying. We've gone over how to beat procrastination, how to read and take notes, how to build your environment, stay organized, plan well, etc.

However, *this* step will focus on the actual act of sitting down and attempting to permanently encode information you've already learned once into your brain.

Replicate the Test Conditions

This may seem like an obvious question, but ask yourself: *Why are you studying?* You're going through your classes and major because there's a specific set of information and skills you want to learn... but there's a more **pressing** reason as to why you need to study *now.*

That reason is the **assessment.** Your immediate need to learn and remember certain material from your classes stems from the quizzes, exams, and essays you'll face later on. You can take advantage of this fact by attempting to **replicate the test conditions** when you study. If you can simulate your exams during your study sessions, then you'll experience much less anxiety and be far more prepared when you actually walk into your tests.

Here's a simple process for doing this:

Step 1: Gather Your Materials

Hopefully your organization skills (built in Step 6) will make this easy. To get started, pull together any and all class documents, notes, and learning materials that pertain to the test. These include:

- Your syllabus, assuming it includes assignments/readings/test details
- Class handouts
- Lecture slides, if they're available to you
- Your own notes
- Homework assignments
- Your textbook

Now your ammo is well-stocked. Time to formulate a

plan of attack.

Step 2: Identify What's Important and Build a Study Guide

Use the details from your syllabus and other materials handed out by your professor to start making a list of the **most important topics** that you think will be covered on the test. You should also review your notes and look for the top-level terms and concepts that were covered in class - these will probably show up on your test.

Your syllabus may provide hints by listing topics covered in class, specific reading assignments, etc. - so make sure you consult this as well.

If your professor happened to provide a *study guide* for the test, this is the equivalent to a bar of gold. Actually, gold isn't all that useful in an objective sense... ok, it's even more useful. In my experience, study guides from your professor are often an outline of *exactly* the material you'll be tested on. I vividly remember going through my Human Sexuality study guides, only to show up on test days and realize my exams were basically exact copies of said study guides. I should have brought one of those Easy Buttons to class with me.

Assuming your professor doesn't just hand you the keys to the kingdom in the form of a study guide, **it's**

time to make your own. Start looking at your list of important topics, terms, and concepts you put together, and turn those into a list of **questions** that will force you to recall the information *actively* (more about this in the next section).

Think of yourself as an army for the purposes of this study session; right now, you're a team of **drill designers.** You're currently designing the combat drills that your soldiers will run through in order to build the muscle memory, team dynamics, and keen judgement required to be effective in a real combat situation.

If your army doesn't run through drills, or if the drills don't closely match what they'll find in real combat, then they won't be well prepared. That's why it's important to try, as closely as you can, to mirror the format of the exam when you study.

You can even play with other factors, such as the location and time constraints, once you've gained a solid grasp on the material. For big tests, it's often worth doing a final practice run to make sure you're ready. Remember this:

> *"The mark of good learning isn't that you got it right; it's that you can't get it wrong."*

The closer your study conditions are to your test conditions, the more you'll be able to *reduce your anxiety* come test day. This is **vital,** as anxiety actually *blocks* your ability to recall information easily. If you've **mastered** the material, however, you can overcome this anxiety. And, if you've already experienced similar conditions to what you're facing during the test, that anxiety might not creep up as badly in the first place.

Step 3: Get to Studying

Now, get to work. Use your procrastination-fighting techniques, and maybe even a bit of timeboxing, to force yourself to study. Fill out your study guide by actively answering the questions you created earlier. Test yourself until recalling the material is easy.

Godspeed, friend.

Emphasize Active Learning

I've had friends who would "study" for a test by opening the lecture slides and lazily scrolling through them. I'm not sure if they were hoping to learn by osmosis or something, but *spoilers*... it didn't work well.

Passive Learning - simply trying to expose yourself to information in the hopes that it'll "sink in" somehow - isn't very effective. Your brain learns best when it's forced to *do* things - work out hard problems, recall previous information it learned, etc.

This is called **Active Learning,** and it should form the basis of all your studying efforts. This starts with active reading, as I talked about in Step 3 - you should go through your reading assignments intently, either by highlighting, taking notes, or summarizing what you read.

Your proclivity towards active modes of learning should then extend to your studying and review sessions. This is another huge reason I showed you the process in the last step - the act of gathering your materials, creating a study guide from them, and then answering those questions (essentially quizzing yourself) is all part of learning actively.

Use Spaced Repetition

When it comes to learning lots of individual facts and pieces of data - vocab terms, foreign language words, definitions - **spaced repetition** is one of the most efficient techniques for getting them into your long-term memory quickly.

Spaced repetition is a learning technique that encourages you to study the things you're good at *less* often, while quizzing you on the things you're bad at *more* often. As you study, a spaced repetition system will record your performance on each item and define a period of waiting before showing you that item again. If you find it easy to recall the information, you won't see it for a long time; if it's difficult, you may see it multiple times in the same study session.

This benefits you in two ways:

- You efficiently spend your study time on the things you still need help learning
- Your brain is forced to recall each item at the point where it's closest to forgetting it

The harder your brain has to work to recall something, the more useful that instance of recalling it is.

Spaced repetition studying is most often carried out with flashcards, and the most useful program for practicing it is called <u>Anki</u>. This app is available for every major platform as well as on the web, and it lets you create "decks" of cards that you study just like paper flashcards.

Anki also has a large bank of shared decks made by others, which you can definitely peruse. However, I do think it's very useful to create your own decks, as the act of creating study materials exposes your brain to the material in a different context - creation instead of review. This, in turn, helps you become even *more* familiar with it. Remember those professors that let you fill out a single notecard for use on a test? The kids that spent all night trying to cram their entire textbook onto the notecard in uber-tiny handwriting ended up learning a lot of that material in the process. Creating your own flashcard decks has a similar effect.

As you study with Anki, you'll provide it with a difficulty rating for each flashcard once you reveal its answer. Anki will take these ratings and use them to figure out how long to wait before showing you that card again.

Anki takes advantage of the **spacing effect,** which is a phenomenon in our brains that makes it easier to remember information that is presented in multiple, spaced-out study sessions rather than one huge cramming session. As a result, Anki is at its best when you start using it early and regularly. While you can fiddle with its settings to help with late-night cramming sessions, it won't be as useful. Hopefully, though, your planning skills will eliminate the need to do this very often!

How to Study Math (and Similar Subjects)

Subjects like history are like jigsaw puzzles; you can start almost anywhere, and as you learn, you'll eventually piece together individual pieces of information and stories into one big, cohesive whole. By that analogy, though, subjects like math are like a **house.**

There's a definite place you should start, and each new concept you learn *builds upon the last*. This means that you need a solid understanding of each concept before you move onto the next.

> *"Each truth that I discovered became a rule which then served to discover other truths."* - Rene Descartes

To learn math effectively, you have to account for this fact when studying it. You can't tackle it like other subjects; building an Anki deck for math terms and calling it a day isn't going to help you much when you're trying to complete a math test. To that end, here are the tips I have for your math studies:

1. Learn to notice your confusion
2. Understand, don't memorize
3. Do. The. Math.

Learning to Notice Confusion

You're going to spend a lot of time confused when you're learning math. However, due to the breakneck pace of most math classes, you may not always notice exactly *where* your confusion stems from - you might look at an example problem, understand most of the process that led to the answer, and simply decide that it "makes sense" at the time.

When you find yourself thinking that something

"makes sense," it's probably a good time to challenge that assumption. Can you take a similar problem and work it out to get a correct solution? Many times, you'll try this and find that you get stuck at a certain point when your professor isn't there to guide you through it. You've learned part of the process; as one Stanford math professor said, you've gained some tendrils of knowledge that extend away from your comfort zone. Now, you need to "backfill" - go back and fill in the gaps that remain. Learning math in a completely systematic way, where you understand every concept perfectly before moving to the next, is almost impossible. This "backfilling" is necessary for you to be able to move on.

Understand, Don't Memorize

This goes right back to what I mentioned about *mastery* in a previous section; however, with math, it's doubly important. In math, you need to understand *why* operations work the way they do. You need to grok the *underlying logic* behind the concepts you're learning.

When you do this, you no longer need to memorize things. Memorizing can help you fit shaped blocks into similar-shaped holes that you've seen before - "Ok, I know *x* goes *here* in this equation because I saw it before..." - but understanding will give you the ability to tackle problems with details you haven't seen before. A core understanding of the fundamentals makes it possible to deal with new things.

You should be shooting for the, "Aha!" moments. Let's step back from math for a second to take a look at another subject I've spent a lot of time in - programming. As a web developer, I've had to get my hands dirty with several different programming languages, as well as frameworks that build upon those languages and add their own constructs and shortcuts.

When you're learning a new language, you don't understand it. However, you're still able to look at the source code for a particular program or web page, look then to the actual product, and see that it works. You could just memorize the exact code and type something similar later on to get the same result - but you don't actually understand *why* it's giving you that particular output. You can't follow the logic of the code yet.

Since web development was my job, though, I *needed* to know the "why." It was my job to use these tools to create new projects with different features, so I needed to understand the underlying logic. Eventually, after spending hours pouring over existing code, tinkering and changing things, reading through documentation, and asking for help, it'd finally "click" and I'd say:

"Ooooooohhhhh!!!!"

These are the moments you should seek when studying math. If you don't understand a concept well enough to work problems that use it, you need to keep pushing until that concept "clicks." Your goal is true understanding, not mere memorization.

A good rule of thumb for gauging understanding is the "Explanation Test." If your kid brother asked you about the concept you're studying, could you adequately explain it to him? Could you work through an example problem with him and tell him *why* each step happened the way it did? If not, you have more work to do.

Do. The. Math!

In high school, my idea of studying math was sitting back in my chair and watching the teacher go through example problems on the board. During class, I'd watch him go through each step and think, "Yeah, that makes sense. I could do this myself."

Here's the thing: Sitting back in your chair and watching your teacher do math makes you good at... sitting back in your chair and watching your teacher do math.

Math is not a spectator sport. While you're in class, you should strive to record as much detail as possible in your notes - including the fully worked-out versions of practice problems - because later you need to hunker down and actually **do problems** on your own.

Math is all about going through the actual procedures, working the problems, and getting your hands dirty with the concepts and rules. During math tests, you won't spend much of your time answering true/false questions about math concepts. Learn their definitions, yes - but spend most of your time working out problem after problem after problem. *This* is what you'll have to do during a test, and the only way you're going to get good at it is *practice.*

In addition to doing lots of problems though, you can also **seek help.** Ask your professors, form a study group, or use one of these online resources (they're certainly not the only ones):

- <u>Wolfram Alpha</u> - type a math problem into the search bar and it'll both solve it *and* give you the steps. Don't use this as a crutch.
- <u>Mathematics Stack Exchange</u> - a great place for asking math-specific questions.
- <u>r/homeworkhelp</u> - a subreddit dedicated to helping people with homework problems.

I'll mention one last thing: The scope of this book isn't big enough to cover individual math topics, but you *should* make sure you're clear on things like notation, order of operations (PEMDAS does *not* mean you do multiplication before division; don't let me catch you doing it), etc. Also, check your work on tests. You *will* make dumb errors at times.

STEP 9: WRITE BETTER PAPERS

On my first day of 10th grade, I walked into Mrs. Coover's *Honors English I* class and expected it to be a complete cakewalk, much like every other English class I had ever taken.

Five minutes later, she announced,

> *"Each of you has six essays to write by the end of the week."*

Jaws dropped. Eyes bulged. Incredulity became more than a shared mental state; it became a tangible part of the atmosphere itself. You could breathe it.

Of course, none of us died. Writing six essays was tough, and the class remained difficult for the rest of the semester - but we made it through, and with incredibly improved writing skills to boot.

Due in part to the solid foundation Mrs. Coover's class gave me, writing a 5-page paper is no longer a daunting task for me. This section of the book will attempt to make it a bit less daunting for you as well.

Do a Brain Dump

Your process for completing a writing assignment should start out much like any other assignment; you'll use the skills you learned from Step 6 to gather all the relevant materials and instructions you need to plan out the project and make sure you know all the criteria.

After that, it's time to do a **brain dump.**

This entails thinking about your paper's topic, and then vomiting out everything that comes to mind onto a piece of paper (or an Evernote note). Include:

- Everything you know about the topic
- Questions you have
- Points you think you might like to cover
- Outside sources you'd like to research
- Quotes from others that come to mind

The brain dump is completely unstructured. Your resulting document should look like a mess, because it's a direct representation of what's in your head right now - a messy, unfocused jumble of ideas and questions.

Once you've got that jumble in a safe, permanent place, you can start on the next phase of the process.

Develop a Focus and Key Questions

Now that you've done your brain dump, the next major task you'll be undertaking is **research**.

However, you should first take some time to do two things:

- Develop a well-defined **focus** for your paper
- Come up with several **guiding questions** that you'd like to answer

Research is messy, and if you're not focused, it's going to take you a lot longer to extract meaningful information from your sources.

By developing a focus, you're giving yourself **direction** with your research. It'll also help you to *stay on-point* later when you're writing. My friend Ransom Patterson mentioned in a guest post on CIG that many students make the mistake of not having a clear point when writing their papers; you want to make sure you don't make this mistake.

By taking the time to come up with questions you'd like to answer about your topic, you're creating little mini-goals you'll have in mind while reading. Have you ever tried to look at your surroundings and pick out every object of a certain color? Interestingly, if you close your eyes and focus your mind on that color first, things of that color will stand out much more prominently when you look around again. You've primed your brain to notice that color. Writing questions has a similar priming effect on your brain when you're doing research, so don't skip out on it.

Conduct Better Research

Alright, it's time to stalk to aisles of the library like a wraith... right? Well, yes - but I'd like to help you minimize your time as a wraith and make it as effective as possible.

Cal Newport's book *How to Become a Straight-A Student* has an entire chapter dedicated to research (which I recommend checking out), but I just want to point out a couple things from it here.

The first is that many students get caught up in what he calls **research recursion syndrome** - the "unhealthy need to find yet another source" which can lead to hours of wasted time.

The second is his method for avoiding this, which he sums up by saying, "Research like a machine." This research process is a simple algorithm:

- Find sources
- Make personal copies of all sources
- Annotate the material
- Decide if you're done

Now, before I give you my take on the first step of this process, do me a favor - check to make sure no professors are looking over your shoulder.

Are we good? Ok.

To start finding sources, **use Wikipedia**. Yep. The actual articles on Wikipedia are generally very good, but what you're looking for here are the *sources at the bottom of the page.*

Wikipedia has rigorous standards for the sources of its articles, which means that those sources are often good enough for your papers.

You can also do this with general textbooks and other books such as popular science books. If you look in the back, you're likely to find a detailed bibliography that'll lead you to much more specific and useful texts.

Beyond that, you can still use journal databases and

Google Scholar to find even more sources.

Once, you've found a source, you want to save it in a place where it can be easily managed. For this, I recommend using **Evernote**.

I had a notebook for every class in Evernote as a student, and I highly recommend that you do the same if you use the app. However, if you have a writing project that requires a **lot** of research, you might want to actually create an entire notebook for it.

When you find an online source, you can use Evernote's Web Clipper to save the entire article into your research notebook. When you're dealing with print sources, you can photocopy relevant pages and upload them to your notebook via your computer, or use the Evernote app (or something even faster like Scanbot) to take a picture with your smartphone and import it.

Annotation shouldn't be thought-of as full-blown note-taking; you've got the sources available, so don't worry about taking super-detailed notes. Rather, I recommend skimming your sources quickly and creating short notes that reference page numbers. For online sources you've clipped, Evernote has a handy highlighting feature that works well.

That last step of the process, deciding if you're done,

is quite personal. Cal's suggestion is to list out all the main facts and points that are crucial to support your thesis and make sure you've got at least two sources for each. For topics that might not be crucial, but that you still might like to add, try to have at least one source.

Write an Awful First Draft

Perfectionism is paralyzing. When you think you need to write something amazing the first time your hands start pressing keys, your brain will freeze up and you won't be able to write anything. Unfortunately, this is all too often the state of mind we goal-minded individuals find ourselves in; we simply want to put out great work.

The cure for this? **Write awful first drafts.**

Relegate yourself to knowing that your first attempt at writing something will yield a result that's less than stellar. Be ok with that; you'll be editing and revising later.

Earnest Hemingway didn't say:

> *"Write drunk; edit sober."*

…but people think he did, and regardless of who said it, it's a fitting quote for this section. Write "drunk".

Write like you're one of the DragonForce guitarists, noodling out a random crazy solo without any forethought. Write like you're dancing with the girl of your dreams and you're spinning her around and she's smiling so brightly and you absolutely can't stop to think about how silly you must look because then you'd trip and the whole thing would end.

Yeah. Write like that.

Writing your first draft has a similar purpose to doing the brain dump. **It's all about simply getting your ideas out onto paper.**

Your first draft has the added purpose of adding some structure to those ideas, but it's not the time to be carefully thinking about prose style and document structure and all that jazz.

When you write this awful, terrible, no-good first draft, write it in a place where you're **not emotionally invested**. This means either:

- Writing in a document separate from the one that'll become your final paper
- Writing in an entirely different application

I do a lot of my awful writing in Evernote. I actually have a "Daily Writing" notebook, where I try to simply vomit out words on a prompt every morning. These words will eventually become beautifully crafted blog posts, book chapters, and videos - but in Evernote, there's no pressure for them to look good right away. I know Evernote isn't where I'll publish the final product, so I don't care if the writing there isn't polished.

Other times, I'll do my awful writing in <u>Byword</u>, which is a beautiful, distraction-free writing app for the Mac.

Finally, don't be afraid to meta-write; to **write about the writing**. On many days, I'll start my daily writing session with a paragraph or two about how tired I am or how much I *don't* want to write. I'll write stupid things. Sometimes I'll write little offshoots after a particular sentence - *"Ok Tom, you definitely can't leave this in because you'll look like a prat" - things that keep the stream of consciousness flowing.

Edit Ruthlessly

Stephen King's *On Writing: A Memoir of the Craft* contains a great quote:

> *"Kill your darlings, kill your darlings, even when it breaks your egocentric little scribbler's heart, kill your darlings."*

Your awful first draft truly was awful. Sometimes,

you'll know this right away. Other times, you'll have a hard time believing it because by golly, you were **in the zone** that time! Right? Right???

Here's the truth: No matter how you feel about your first draft, editing can always improve it. Much of the writing *you* think is great will not elicit the same opinion from your readers.

That's why Stephen King tells you to "kill your darlings" - the sentences, paragraphs, and sometimes entire sections that sounded good at first, but that don't pull their weight upon more careful inspection.

Now, editing isn't *only* about cutting things out. Editing is simply the process of revising your paper to make it better. That means adding needed detail, restructuring and reordering your points, and fixing mistakes as well.

I see editing as a two-phase process. In the first phase, you need to answer the *really important* questions:

- Does my paper have good narrative flow?
- Do I have a clear main idea, and does that idea match up with the assignment?
- Does each section back up the main idea in a meaningful way?
- Is each section filled out with ample research?

- What can be removed or stated in a simpler, better manner?

Essentially, this first phase is all about ensuring that your paper is **effectively communicating your main idea** in a way that will keep the reader interested and on-track.

At this point, the technical bits are not important. Don't get hung up on spelling, grammar, sentence structure, or whether or not you're supposed to indent paragraphs.

Instead, read through your draft and ensure that each argument you present backs up the main idea. If one isn't essential - if it needlessly bloats the paper - cut it.

On the other hand, maybe you'll find that you didn't flesh out an essential argument well enough; in that case, go back and add the needed points from your research. Also, think about the **order** of your arguments as well; think about how their placement affects the flow of the paper.

Side note: Since 95% of my writing over the past several years has been for blog posts and other independent projects, I almost forgot about this... but I suppose it's likely that you'll have several writing assignments that have an arbitrary length requirement. (Bleh)

If that's the case, I'd recommend keeping the sections you cut during the editing process in a backup document. Try to hit the length requirement with your essential arguments as best as you can, but if it doesn't work, adding one of those lesser arguments might be justifiable. It's probably a better idea than padding your other arguments with excessive wordiness.

Once you're happy with the narrative structure of your paper, it's time to move on to the second phase of editing: **technical edits.**

At this stage, you're looking through your paper for things like:

1. Spelling and grammar mistakes
2. Badly structured sentences
3. Sentences/paragraphs that don't sound right
4. Formatting errors

Here are a couple of useful tips for making the process of technical editing go more smoothly.

First, **print out your paper.** I find that proofreading my writing in its final intended medium helps me pay closer attention to the details.

For example, each week I send an email newsletter to my readers that updates them on that week's new video and podcast episode. Before sending it, I always email myself a test version and proofread it right in my inbox; often, I catch mistakes I didn't see when going over it in MailChimp's editor. My inbox represents the final medium for the newsletter, and a physical sheet of paper does the same for your writing assignment.

Also, you get an additional benefit by proofreading on paper: **you can only mark the errors.** You can't pause to fix them like you can when you're editing on a computer. I think it's more effective to set your brain to "find what's wrong" mode first, only switching over to "fix the mistakes" mode once you've identified them all. Constantly switching modes can cause mental fatigue, which leads to lazier editing later on in your paper.

Second, **read your paper out loud.** Doing this forces you to slow down as you go over the text, which will allow you to catch more errors. It'll also help you identify any sentences or sections that sound awkward.

Lastly, **take note of your common errors.** Maybe you happen to mix up "their" and "they're" often. Maybe you're not always clear on when to use a comma and when to use a semicolon. Maybe you type really quickly and sometimes leave the "s" off of words that are supposed to be plural.

Whatever your common errors are, it's a good idea to write them down somewhere (perhaps an Evernote document). When you proofread, quickly remind yourself of those common errors so you can more easily spot them.

Alright, we've made it through both phases of the editing process. To round this chapter out, I want to offer up a couple more thoughts that might prove to be helpful.

The first has to do with **getting feedback.** Having other people read through your paper is incredibly helpful, and you can have them do it at pretty much any part of the editing process.

Before you go throwing copies of your paper at all your friends, though, here are a couple pieces of advice you should consider from Microsoft researcher Simon Peyton Jones (who gave an excellent talk on writing research papers):

1. **Each person can read your paper for the first time only once!** Use them carefully. Don't use up all your potential reviewers at the same time; show your paper to one, make changes based on their feedback, and then show it to another.
2. **Explain exactly what kind of feedback you want.** For the most part, feedback like, "I got lost here," or, "The second section was really boring," is much more useful than, "You spelled 'amphibian' wrong."

Also, be aware that both **experts** and **non-experts** make great reviewers. Experts know the subject matter well, so they can point out areas where you're wrong or need to back up your arguments with more evidence. Non-experts can tell you if your paper clearly explains those arguments in an easy-to-follow way.

Finally, after you've finished all your in-depth editing and have had your paper reviewed, print out the final draft and do one final read-through. This time, read the paper all the way through and commit your mind to answering just one question, "Is this paper ready?"

As Cal Newport puts it:

> "The goal of this final pass is to experience your work in one uninterrupted flow. To savor your arguments. To experience the work in the same way your professor will."

Once you're satisfied with that final pass, call it a day. Your paper's most likely destined for an excellent grade.

STEP 10: MAKE GROUP PROJECTS SUCK LESS

My best friend Martin is an absolute champ. During his last year of college, he decided to condense all his remaining classes into a single semester so he could graduate early. Not only that, but he also landed an awesome internship with a company that doesn't normally hire interns.

In addition to working 20 hours a week at that internship, he also spent 6 hours a week commuting to it since it was an hour away from our apartment. Still, he held it down marvelously while completing his remaining classes.

Given that, I think the gods of academia owe him a sincere apology. Why?

Because, again and again over the semester, Martin's professors kept heaping group project after group project on him without end. Eventually, he got them all done - but they definitely took their toll.

My point here is that **group projects suck**. They're terrible. Out of any given group you'll be assigned, it'll probably include:

- The one who pretends to contribute by asking lots of questions, but who never does anything
- The one who has absolutely no idea what is going on and wasn't even in class during the project's introduction
- The one who thinks having 500 in-person meetings a week qualifies as "progress" and wants you to walk 3 miles back to campus at 8 p.m. on a Tuesday night to "make sure we're all on the same page," but doesn't even have his part of the rough draft done
- The one who quickly realizes their future will be partly determined by these people and must relegate themselves to doing all the work - AKA **you**

And, of course, one person in the group will suggest you all communicate via email. You'll agree, only to later find out that everyone else in your group is terrible at responding to their email.

As you tear your hair out at 11:58, waiting for your last group member to send you their part of the project so you can turn it in before the midnight deadline, it dawns on you…

This is but a taste of the real world that awaits you.

Your ridiculous backup plan of becoming a mountain man in the backwoods of the Yukon starts to seem like a tantalizing option now. You can almost taste the beaver meat and the glorious, solitary work of simple survival.

I, too, have dreamt those dreams. I, too, have watched hours of Wranglerstar videos on YouTube, trying to learn how to use a woodsman's axe sans the requisite years of experience.

Before you give in, though, let's see if we can make those group projects suck a little less.

Note: A beta reader suggested that, if you find this chapter useful, you might also want to check out Episode 42 of the CIG podcast, in which my friend Martin and I discuss how to deal with group projects.

Make Good Use of the First Meeting

For almost every group project I ever had to take part in, the group got to meet for a little while during class once the details of the project had been presented. In almost all of these cases, the meetings went like this:

> *"You guys are my group? Cool. Let's bail out early today and agree to meet up sometime next week to plan how we'll do the project. What are your email addresses? Just write them down on this torn up napkin I found in the dumpster earlier and I'll hit you guys up later with deets."*

Now, I know the temptation to leave class early is great, but *please don't do this.* Utilizing the in-class time for this first meeting well can make your project go so much more smoothly.

- Everyone in the group is already present
- The details of the project are fresh in everyone's mind
- Any relevant hand-outs haven't had time to be lost yet

This first in-class meeting is your best opportunity to ~~assert your dominance by peeing on everyone~~ get to know everyone a bit, set up goals and expectations, and create strong communication channels.

During this first meeting, you should get everyone introduced and make sure to get everyone's contact information, including phone numbers if you can and they're all comfortable with it. Also make sure to note down names and email addresses.

Also, you might need to blackmail them into doing your dirty work for you later in life, so make sure you get the names of their family members, their blood type, and their entire web browsing history. This paragraph is satire.

Don't just write down the contact info; enter it into the system you'll be using to communicate and make sure everyone in the group can access it *before* you leave class.

Other things you'll want to do:

- Set up the collaboration and communication systems you'll be using (I'll go over my recommendations in a later section).
- Have everyone candidly tell the group what their strengths, weaknesses, likes, dislikes, etc. are.
- Discuss goals for the project and, if you have enough details and time, create some rough project milestones. If you're suitably Machiavellian, you'll structure your deadlines ahead of schedule to take advantage of the psychology of urgency. If you're suitably nerdy, you might even start creating Gantt charts.

- Assign initial tasks to your group members based on their strengths and preferences. Some might be ok with taking on more work if it's work they prefer, so if that one dude wants to do *all* the coding and none of the paper, it's probably a good idea to let him.

Also, make a *genuine effort* to get at least a little bit acquainted with the people in your group. You don't have to become best friends with them, but at least knowing their majors and making a bit of small talk can go a long way.

Lastly, if you can, set a time for the next meeting while everyone is there.

Avoid the Bystander Effect

The Bystander Effect is a curious bug in the human brain that makes it less likely for any individual to pitch in where help is needed if other people happen to be standing around.

> *"I'm sure someone else will take care of it,"*
> *said everyone ever.*

While this effect is most often associated with emergencies and crimes-in-progress, it also rears its lazy head during group projects if you're not deliberate about assigning tasks. If there's some part of the project that isn't explicitly assigned, your group members may just assume that someone else will take care of it.

This leads up to an inevitable piece of advice for anyone responsible enough to read an entire book on earning better grades... *When in doubt, be the leader.*

Even if you don't fancy yourself a project manager, it's usually best to take up that mantle if no one else seems enthusiastic. Do you already take care of your own calendar and task list diligently? Did you actually implement the advice from Steps 4 and 6?

If so, you're leader material and you should probably just step up and volunteer to run the organization systems, assign the tasks, and be the person who ultimately turns in the project.

Bonus: If the project is substantial enough, you can actually list it as experience on a resume! This tip comes from Brad Karsh, an experienced former recruiting director who read over 10,000 resumes and wrote the book *Confessions of a Recruiting Director*, which I highly recommend.

Solutions vs. Mixtures

Back to 6th grade science class we go! Remember the difference between **mixtures** and **solutions?**

- Mixtures are a unification of materials that retain their physical properties when mixed together. Like fruit salad, yummy yummy.
- Solutions actually change the physical properties of the materials they're made up of, rendering them inseparable by most physical means

You want your group project to be a **solution** - each component should meld perfectly with the others, creating a well-executed final product. Too often, though, groups create patchwork projects that are not tightly integrated. It's very obvious that each group member just went off and did their portion alone, with the final product being slapped together at the last minute.

That's why your group needs an **editor.** Someone should be assigned to collect all the finished components and integrate them nicely together. This editor should pay attention to:

- Writing style and voice (it can be different, but not drastically different, from group member to group member)
- Transitions and consistency between the intro and outro
- Other formatting consistency
- Slide layout/design
- Making sure each member shows up to presentation day dressed at a similar level

To make the editor's job easier, the final deadline for each group member's assignments should be *well* before the actual due date of the project. This will also help to prevent people from being straight-up late with their work.

Use Great Tools to Be More Effective

This is the part you've really been waiting for, right? The part where I tell you about wonderful apps that'll make group projects nothing but sunshine and rainbows?

Cool. That's exactly what I'll do here.

I've been experimenting with collaboration tools ever since high school, when I pissed off my fellow Business Professionals of America officers by trying to get them to use Basecamp. I guess they just wanted to stick with email.

Eight years later, I'm of the same opinion I was back then: **email sucks.** It's a never-ending hydra that's already tough enough to do battle with; you don't need team communication clogging it up further. It wasn't built for managing projects.

The apps I'm about to suggest, however, *were.*

Here's an overview (all are free):

- **Trello:** Project/task management
- **Slack:** Team communication
- **Google Docs:** Collaborative writing, file sharing

Trello

Trello is my absolute favorite app for managing projects of any kind. It utilizes **Kanban cards,** which are part of a Japanese project management system developed at Toyota. This system lets you easily track the status of any task in a project, and Trello adds in lots of other useful features.

When I hired Martin to help code the redesigned version of my website back in late 2013, we set up a Trello board for the project. It was *massively* helpful, as there were a ton of things to keep track of.

On a Trello board, you can create any number of lists, which in turn can hold any number of cards. Typically, a project will utilize these features like so:

- **Lists** will describe the stages of the project - Planning, In Progress, On Hold, Done
- **Cards** describe actual tasks that need to be done

As progress is made on tasks, you'll move the cards from list to list until they're done.

Trello also lets you assign individual cards to members who are part of the board, so it's really easy to delegate tasks and see, at a glance, who's doing what.

Cards themselves are powerful as well; each card can hold notes, screenshots, attachments of any kind, and even tasks lists - which are good for breaking tasks down in to actionable steps.

Slack

Slack is, in my opinion, the best team chat/comm-unication app out there. It combines IRC-style "channels," which are chat rooms visible to everyone on the Slack team, with options for private groups and direct messages.

The great thing about Slack is that it removes the verbosity of email; it's easy to pop in, ask a question, and get an answer - just like you'd do over text or Facebook.

However, it also includes a ton of integrations and great notification settings. There are apps for OS X, Android, and iOS, as well as a great web app. For my Slack team, which is quite large at this point, I've set it up so that I'll get notified on my phone if I either get a direct message or have my username mentioned in any channel (a la Twitter notifications).

As for integrations, there are tons of apps you can connect to Slack - including Trello and Google Docs. This makes it the perfect "home base" of sorts for your team. You can configure the Trello integration so that a Slack channel is updated whenever cards are moved on Trello, and as project manager you can set up notifications for that channel so you stay up to date on the progress of the project.

The only real downside to Slack, honestly, is that you'll want to use it for *all* your online communication after getting used to it. It's that good.

Google Docs

Out of any app I'll recommend here, I'll assume you're the most familiar with Google Docs. It's probably just as well-known as Microsoft Office at this point.

For writing the first draft of your papers, though, I highly recommend using it over Word. Group members can collaborate on the same document at the same time, and it's ridiculously easy to open up said document to review changes. Downloading a Word doc is much less convenient.

You can also use Google Drive as a shared file storage space for any assets/research your team needs to share during the project. Personally, I use Dropbox for most of my team file sharing, but Drive is generally easier to convince group members to use since they likely have a Gmail account already.

FIN: WHERE TO GO FROM HERE

Whew! We've covered a ton of information in this book, and we're finally finished. Perhaps now you're wondering:

"What should I do now?"

To start, I suggest you identify 1-2 **main focuses** of improvement that you'd like to work on in your own life as a student. Maybe you'd like to get more organized, or start becoming a better planner. Perhaps you'd like to start learning more efficiently.

Whatever it is, *write down a goal* and then form a plan of action for achieving it.

Beyond that, here are a few things I'd love for you to do:

- **Review this book on Amazon:** If you have a couple minutes, I would be hugely appreciative if you'd be willing to write an honest review of the book. I'd like to write a second book in the future, and every review of this one will help publishers decide if they'd like to work with me. If you do, thank you!

- **Join the CIG newsletter:** If you'd like to get email updates about the videos, podcast episodes, and blog posts I create (as well as super secret future projects), this is the best way to do it. You'll also get some free bonus resources, including my graduation planning Excel template.

- **Want me to come speak at your school?** That link will take you to my speaking page; sending it to an academic success coordinator or a professor at your school and letting them know about my work can help get the ball rolling.

I'd also just like to say *thank you* for reading this far. I truly hope you'll be able to apply the advice in this book and become a more efficient student.

Lastly, I'll note that studying is not my only focus on College Info Geek. It's also my goal to help you **impress recruiters, land the job of your dreams,** and **destroy your student debt.**

If you'd like to check out the videos, podcast episodes, and articles that are already on the site, <u>check out my list of the best posts</u>.

WHO AM I?

If this book is your introduction to College Info Geek, you might be wondering what makes me think I can tell you how to go about your studies.

Well, in short, it's good 'ole fashioned audacity.

In truth, I don't believe anyone can or will ever be a monopolistic force in determining how you approach your studying - or anything else. Smart people learn from many sources, pick specific pieces and tidbits, experiment with them, and gradually form their own mental encyclopedia of "Stuff That Works."

Here's why I'd like you to consider adding what I've written in this book into your STW archives. *If you're familiar with Aristotle's three artistic proofs, this'd be the Ethos.*

My name's Thomas Frank, and I've been writing about how to be awesome at college for over six years now. I live in Iowa, have an awe-inspiring beard, and graduated with a degree in MIS from Iowa State University in 2013.

As a student, I was *laser-focused* on making my college experience a remarkable one - and my end goal was to build up enough knowledge, skills, and connections that I'd **never** face a situation where I didn't have career options.

To that end, I started reading about productivity and efficient learning systems. I also tried to gain lots of experience in a lot of different areas and to push myself out of my comfort zone on a regular basis.

A few of the things that happened as a result:

1. I graduated with a 3.46 GPA without ever needing to study more than a few hours a week (considering my other commitments, this was my personal definition of awesome grades).
2. As a sophomore, I found myself with 7 interview requests from different companies even before the fall career fair started.
3. The company I interned for (a Fortune 500) offered me an internship without interviewing me.

4. I was able to work 20 hours/week during most semesters, which meant I never felt broke.

5. In March of 2013 - two months before I graduated - I finished paying off $14,431 in student loans.

During the summer following my freshman year, I was politely rejected when I applied to write for a large college success blog I'd been following. Unwilling to let the article I'd written for them go to waste, I taught myself how to install WordPress and put up a little blog called College Info Geek.

Six years later, CIG attracts over 250,000 students every month. The site has over 600 articles on studying better, becoming more productive, landing internships and jobs, and mastering money.

In addition to the research that went into all those articles and my own personal experiments in learning and productivity, I've also learned from true experts in numerous fields through the conversations I've had on the College Info Geek podcast - a weekly show that interviews successful students, professors, entrepreneurs, and other really smart people on learning, productivity, career advice, and more.

Lastly, I also create weekly videos at the College Info Geek YouTube channel, which has over 300,000 subscribers.

If you'd like to connect with me, I'm @TomFrankly on Twitter and would love to hear from you. Feel free to send me any questions you have, and also let me know what you thought of this book!

SPECIAL THANKS

Huge thank you to all the students who helped me edit the first draft of this book!

- Ransom P.
- Victoria C.
- Clayton B.
- Audrey C.

Cover icon credits:

- "Coffee" symbol is by Edward Boatman.
- "Book" symbol is by Eugen Belyakoff.
- "Goat" symbol is by Anand Prahlad.
- "Brain" symbol is by anonymous.

All icons are from thenounproject.com.

Made in the USA
San Bernardino, CA
19 December 2016